Clinical Surveillance

The Actionable Benefits of Objective
Medical Device Data for Crucial Decision-Making

Clinical Surveillance

The Actionable Benefits of Objective
Medical Device Data for Crucial Decision-Making

John R. Zaleski, Ph.D., NREMT

CRC Press
Taylor & Francis Group
Boca Raton London New York

CRC Press is an imprint of the
Taylor & Francis Group, an **informa** business

A PRODUCTIVITY PRESS BOOK

First published 2021
by Routledge
52 Vanderbilt Avenue, New York, NY 10017

and by Routledge
2 Park Square, Milton Park, Abingdon, Oxon, OX14 4RN

Routledge is an imprint of the Taylor & Francis Group, an informa business

© 2021 Taylor & Francis

The right of John R. Zaleski to be identified as author of this work has been asserted by him in accordance with sections 77 and 78 of the Copyright, Designs and Patents Act 1988.

Library of Congress Cataloging-in-Publication Data

A catalog record for this title has been requested

ISBN: 978-0-367-37386-3 (hbk)
ISBN: 978-0-367-36930-9 (pbk)
ISBN: 978-0-429-35344-4 (ebk)

Typeset in Garamond
by Deanta Global Publishing Services, Chennai, India

For Zoey, Isaac, and Cheryl

Contents

List of Figures

List of Tables

Preface

When I started out in my career in the mid-1980s, it was not in the field of medicine or healthcare. I received both my Bachelor of Science and Master of Science in aerospace engineering. I was caught up in the love and excitement of the former Apollo program and the new Space Shuttle program and was "all-in." I went to work for a defense contractor after graduation and got began working in the world of missiles, guidance, spacecraft, and satellites, including electro-optics, radar, and the technologies associated with aircraft and space flight.

As time went on, I developed many software programs and algorithms used for missile and space vehicle tracking, guidance, and target identification. The work was very intense and analytical, involving complex mathematics involving the use of empirically collected data to provide correction to mathematical theory.

During this period, my wife and I were also building a family of two young boys. As with most young families, we were busy with the daily activities of life. While the challenges of being a husband and father were new to me, they were about to become much more complex when my mother phoned me one day to tell me that she had been diagnosed with a very virulent form of inflammatory breast cancer and her prospects were not good. My life suddenly changed in a way I had not anticipated. I took what time I could to visit with her, took her to chemotherapy treatments, engaged her oncologist in discussions about her treatment, and, together with my sister, attempted the best way I knew how to help her. Mom passed away within approximately 18 months of first diagnosis. I will never forget it, and, to this day, I can recount every moment of her illness in my head. That was more than 28 years ago at the time of this writing. The events leading to her death and the arc of her illness forged in me the question about how to detect and monitor changes in patient state for the purpose of identifying how a patient evolves or devolves over time.

My undergraduate training in engineering, and subsequent clinical education and training as an emergency medical technician and ongoing education many years later, framed the concept of an evolving or devolving patient state in my mind. This concept is analogous to the traditional mathematical models representing the state vectors of aircraft or spacecraft in powered and ballistic free flight. Of course, the human body does not conform to precisely the same mathematical behaviors as ballistic flight: in many ways, biological science is much more complex than rocket science. Yet, various human subsystems interact and are integrated with one another, and the interactive behaviors of these subsystems indicate the state of the whole being: a holistic view of the patient as a system. For instance, cardiac and respiratory subsystems are tightly linked, and both depend on and influence one another. The renal, lymphatic, and endocrine subsystems also interact with the cardiac and respiratory subsystems, and their health and well-being or lack thereof influence the others, sometimes in not-soobvious ways.

Clinically, the mechanisms of interaction are important to understand in that the appearance of certain symptoms and findings provides telltale information indicative of whether a specific patient presentation is representative of a particular illness. The data obtained from automated sources, such as physiological monitors, mechanical ventilators, and other monitoring or therapeutic type medical devices (a.k.a. patient care devices), are fairly objective sources of information that establish a "state vector" representative of the current state of the cardiovascular and respiratory subsystems indicating homeostasis, or a tendency towards stability.

It should be noted that physiological monitoring and other types of medical device data, such as from mechanical ventilators, are not error-free: simply, these data sources are fairly objective and data are obtained at regular intervals. Yet, when these objective data are combined with clinical observations, laboratory results, and imaging, a clearer picture of the patient emerges.

Thus, when I was asked by the publisher to consider revising my last book, *Connected Medical Devices: Integrating Patient Care Data in Health Systems* [1], I decided, rather, to focus on the use of medical device data for managing patients clinically, and how these data can be used to tell a story about how the patient is evolving away from, or devolving towards, an adverse event. This vision motivated the writing of this book. Through it, I present the basics of clinical surveillance using real-time data and the potential uses of these data for clinical action. This book "connects the dots" from my previous books related to medical device integration and the use of data for clinical intervention. I have written three books around medical device integration to electronic medical record systems over the course of the past dozen years. My first book on the subject was *Integrating Device Data into the Electronic Medical Record* [2]. In that text, which was the first or seminal text on the topic of medical device integration (MDI), I laid out the technical and workflow considerations of integrating medical device data into the health information system. The book was written just prior to the passage of the American Recovery and Reinvestment Act (ARRA) of 2009, which paved the way for more meaningful health data interoperability and expanded the use of electronic health record systems [3]. The ARRA put forward the concept of Meaningful Use (MU), having five "pillars" [4]:

1. Improving quality, safety, efficiency, and reducing health disparities;
2. Engage patients and families in their health;
3. Improve care coordination;
4. Improve population and public health; and,
5. Ensure adequate privacy and security protection for personal health information.

The MU legislation was published at a time when MDI was still very much a "fringe" activity within health systems. The Meaningful Use Guideline published in the Federal Register, per Section 3004(b)(1) of the PHSA, required "...the Secretary of Health and Human Services ...to adopt an initial set of standards, implementation specifications, and certification criteria ... to enhance the interoperability, functionality, utility, and security of health information technology" [5].

The implementation of requirements was laid out in several steps or stages, with Stage 1 establishing the basis for interoperability. The integration of medical devices into the electronic health record system (EHR) played a large role in MU targets beginning in 2013 through 2015 [6]. That is, meaningful use of an electronic health record (EHR) should include medical device integration and interoperability.

My second book, published in 2011, provided a first treatment on clinical surveillance from the perspective of how to use the data from medical devices to facilitate clinical decision making. That book, *Medical Device Data and Modeling for Clinical Decision Making* [7], was really the predecessor to this one on clinical surveillance.

Finally, in 2015, I followed up with a more operational text: *Connected Medical Devices: Integrating Patient Care Data in Healthcare Systems* [1], which focused on the specifics of acquiring, implementing, configuring, operating, and maintaining a medical device integration deployment, directed toward the healthcare system audience.

After completing that book, I was approached to write a chapter on the subject of Big Data and its uses in healthcare. The result was a book chapter titled "Big Data for Predictive Analytics in High Acuity Health Settings" [8]. Upon completing that chapter, I was motivated to attempt a longer treatment on the topic of clinical surveillance, which led to the current text.

This book is structured in the following way:

- Chapter 1: *Introduction to Clinical Surveillance*, focused on defining it, why is it needed, and why now.
- Chapter 2: *Use of Patient Care Device Data for Clinical Surveillance*—specifically, medical device data obtained through medical device integration.
- Chapter 3: *Alarms and Clinical Surveillance*—how do (or should) medical device alarms play a role in clinical surveillance or is clinical surveillance an entity unto its own that will replace clinical alarms?
- Chapter 4: *Mathematical Techniques Applied to Clinical Surveillance*—data analysis techniques and assessment, including an exposure to some of the methods that providers and researchers can use to assess data obtained from bedside medical devices.
- Chapter 5: *Clinical Workflows Supported by Patient Care Device Data*—scenarios involving the use of patient care device data to help identify adverse events and decompensating patients (note: I will often use the terms *medical device* and *patient care device* interchangeably in the text; my intended meaning is the same).
- Chapter 6: *Epilogue: Lessons Learned from Continuous Monitoring*—examples of several use cases defining the specific what, how, and why of the use of vital signs data to support clinical surveillance.

John R. Zaleski
Elkton, MD

Acronyms

Acronym	Definition
AAMI	Association for the Advancement of Medical Instrumentation
ABG	Arterial Blood Gas
ABP	Arterial Blood Pressure
ACCE	American College of Clinical Engineering
ACM	Alert Communication Management enables the remote communication of point-of-care medical device alert conditions ensuring the right alert with the right priority to the right individuals with the right content (e.g., evidentiary data). It also supports alarm escalation or confirmation based on dissemination status, such as whether the intended clinician has received and acknowledged the condition. (See IHE.NET: https://wiki.ihe.net/index.php/Patient_Care_Device)
AG	Anion Gap
AHRQ	Agency for Healthcare Research and Quality
ALT	Alanine aminotransferase
APSF	Anesthesia Patient Safety Foundation
ARRA	American Recovery and Reinvestment Act
AST	Aspartate aminotransferase
ATP	Adenosine Triphosphate
bpm	Beats per minute
BE	Base Excess
BUN	Blood Urea Nitrogen
Ca^+	Calcium ions

(*Continued*)

Acronym	Definition
CABG	Coronary Artery Bypass Grafting
CBF	Cerebral Blood Flow
CBT	Code Blue Team
CHF	Congestive Heart Failure
Cl⁻	Chlorine ions
cmH$_2$O	Centimeters of water (pressure)
CMP	Comprehensive Metabolic Panel
CNS	Central Nervous System
CO	Cardiac Output
COPD	Chronic Obstructive Pulmonary Disorder
CPAP	Continuous Positive Airway Pressure
CPP	Cerebral Perfusion Pressure
Cr	Creatinine
CT	Computed Tomography
CTEPH	Chronic Thromboembolic Pulmonary Hypertension
CVA	Cerebrovascular accident
CVP	Central Venous Pressure
DEC	Device Enterprise Communication supports publication of information acquired from point-of-care medical devices to applications such as clinical information systems and electronic health record systems, using a consistent messaging format and device semantic content. (See IHE.NET: https://wiki.ihe.net/index.php/Patient_Care_Device)
DTFT	Discrete Time Fourier Transform
DWT	Discrete Wavelet Transform
ECG/EKG	Electrocardiogram
ECRI	Emergency Care Research Institute (formerly); ECRI has been adopted by the Institute as both its name and acronym
ED	Emergency Department
EHR	Electronic Health Record
EMS	Emergency Medical Services

(*Continued*)

Acronym	Definition
etCO$_2$	End-tidal Carbon Dioxide
ETT	Endotracheal Tube or Tubing
EWS	Early Warning Score(s)
FDA	(U.S.) Food and Drug Administration
FFT	Fast Fourier Transform
FiO$_2$	Fraction of Inspired Oxygen
FN	False Negative
FP	False Positive
f_R	Frequency of Respiration (*see Respiration rate*)
FTR	Failure To Rescue
Glu	Serum glucose level
HAI	Hospital Acquired Infections
HCO$_3^-$	Bicarbonate
HIT	Healthcare Information Technology
HL7	Health Level Seven
HR	Heart Rate or Pulse
ICP	Intracranial Pressure
ICU	Intensive Care Unit
IEEE	Institute of Electrical and Electronics Engineering
IHE	Integrating the Healthcare Enterprise
K$^+$	Potassium ions
KF	Kalman Filter
LAN	Local Area Network
LONS	Late-Onset Neonatal Sepsis
LSP	Lomb-Scargle Periodogram
LSSA	Least Squares Spectral Analysis (see LSP)
MAP	Mean Arterial Pressure
MDI	Medical Device Integration

(*Continued*)

Acronym	Definition
MDICC	Medical Device Interoperability Coordinating Council
MET	Medical Emergency Team (See Rapid Response Team)
MIMIC	Medical Information Mart for Critical Care
mmHg	Millimeters of Mercury (pressure)
MR	Magnetic Resonance
MU	Meaningful Use
Na^+	Sodium ions
NBP or NiBP	Non-invasive Blood Pressure
NIF	Negative Inspiratory Force, or Pressure
NIST	National Institute of Science and Technology
NPV	Negative Predictive Value
OIRD	Opioid-Induced Respiratory Depression
OIVI	Opioid-Induced Ventilatory Impairment
OR	Operating Room
$PaCO_2$	Partial pressure of carbon dioxide in blood stream
PaO_2	Partial pressure of oxygen in blood stream
PCA	Patient Controlled Analgesia
PCD	Patient Care Device(s)
PEEP	Positive End-Expiratory Pressure
pH	potential of Hydrogen
PIP	Peak Inspiratory Pressure
POC	Point of Care
PPV	Positive Predictive Value
PR	Pulse Rate
PRN	Pro re nata; as needed
PSD	Power Spectral Density
$PtCO_2$	Partial pressure of carbon dioxide measured via transcutaneous sensor

(*Continued*)

Acronym	Definition
RD	Respiratory Depression
RPM	Respirations per minute
RR	Respiration Rate
RRT	Rapid Response Team
RV	Right Ventricular
SI	Shock Index
SIMV	Synchronous Intermittent Mandatory Ventilation
SIRS	Systemic Inflammatory Response Syndrome
SOAP	Subjective-Objective-Assessment-Plan
SoB	Shortness of Breath
SpO_2	Oxygen hemoglobin percentage measured through pulse oximetry
SVO_2	Venous oxygen saturation, or content
T	Temperature
T_c	Temperature, core
TCA	Total clinically actionable
Thr	Threshold, or threshold value of a parameter
TJC	The Joint Commission
TN	True Negative
TNCA	Total non-clinically actionable
TP	True Positive
TTN	Total test negative
TTP	Total test positive
UOM	Units of Measure
US	Ultrasound
VAP	Ventilator Acquired Pneumonia
V_c	Vital Capacity
$\dot{V}/\dot{Q}$	Ventilation/perfusion

(*Continued*)

Acronym	Definition
V_d/V_T	Dead space fraction
Ve	Minute volume
Vt	Tidal volume
WCM	Waveform Communication Management will extend the DEC profile to provide a method for passing near real-time waveform data using HL7 v2 observation messages. For example, passing wave snippets as evidentiary data in an alarm message communicated using ACM transactions. (See IHE.NET: https://wiki.ihe.net/index.php/Patient_Care_Device)
WoB	Work of Breathing
XR	X Ray

Chapter 1

Introduction to Clinical Surveillance

Clinical Surveillance. What does it mean and why dedicate an entire book to the subject?

Clinical is defined by Merriam-Webster as "of, relating to, or conducted in or as if in a clinic: such as (a) involving direct observation of the patient clinical diagnosis; (b) based on or characterized by observable and diagnosable symptoms" [9].

Surveillance is defined by the same source as *"close watch kept over someone or something (as by a detective)"* [10].

The compound term *Clinical Surveillance* is self-evident by the combination of the terms: the intent is to provide a close and continuous watch over a patient in a clinical setting. The terms together imply a close watch—a continuous watch—over all aspects of the subject patient. The term surveillance has been applied in other domains to imply the same close watch, based on the available information on the subject and the environment in which the subject is active. By analogy, in the context of surveillance as might be considered from a law enforcement or military perspective, the implication is the close observation and oversight of a subject (target) in all its aspects. A key point is that close observation implies *continuous*—that is, uninterrupted observation and monitoring so that the subject of the surveillance is always under scrutiny for changes that may be of interest or import. In a sense, continuous monitoring can seem foreboding—both for the individual performing the surveillance and for the subject of the surveillance—in terms of the energy required to surveil and for possible concerns regarding the "privacy" of the individual being surveilled. Personal privacy implications and continuous surveillance are potentially competing interests that need to be balanced to meet the best interests of both the subject (patient) and the observer (clinician). Yet, in the application of clinical surveillance, the subject or the "target" of the surveillance is the individual patient, and the object is to detect changes in patient "state" or condition that would be deemed untoward or adverse—changes or trends toward the undesirable. Continuous oversight of patients can consume a great deal of energy and time. In certain locations within the healthcare setting (e.g., intensive care units, operating rooms, telemetry units, emergency departments) the effort to oversee patients continuously requires dedicated personnel and equipment that can monitor patient cardiac and respiratory function. In such cases, alarms and notifications surrounding untoward deviations in patient state are transmitted in real-time to inform clinical personnel of adverse events so that rapid intervention can be initiated as required. The annunciation of alarms and alarm signals is a subject of a later chapter relating to detecting and differentiating true alarms from false alarms. Because alarms can become overwhelming in environments such as cardiac telemetry units and intensive care units (ICUs), other aids need to be brought to bear to assist the clinician in the continuous surveillance of patients to help identify when an alarm truly requires immediate action. The physiological monitoring and other equipment employed in these environments enable the setting of alarms or limit settings that identify when undesirable changes happen to a patient, and the changes in patient "state" as measured through physiological parameters provide insight into how patients evolve (or devolve) over time.

Yet, patients are not robots and do not obey absolute guidelines or behaviors in terms of their physiological responses. Those individuals reading this who are licensed clinicians may understand this and also recognize that while patients can present with gross symptoms that are consistent with known diagnoses, variations can exist that either make such diagnoses difficult at first, or make the diagnoses obvious, again, depending on patient presentation. Thus, the key message is that viewing "the numbers" alone—vital signs, for example—is necessary but insufficient in terms of diagnosing a patient. Direct observation combined with other sources of information, including comprehensive metabolic panels, imaging, and direct observation, combined with palpation and auscultation, are necessary and expected as part of clinical practice. The numbers obtained from vital signs measurement, however, can provide an important adjunct for early notification as to a change of state in the patient that could predate adverse events. The identification of these early warning signs is the subject of this text, together with example techniques that can be used to assist in the identification of such events.

1.1 Patient Safety and Clinical Surveillance

It has been estimated that half of reported adverse events, or events leading to decompensation, and upwards of 60% of general care unit patients, experience "at least one or aberrant vital signs measurements up to six hours prior to a cardiac arrest" [11].

In the context of clinical surveillance, a key reason for observing changes in patient state is to identify adverse events early enough so as to be able to ward off or lessen the impact on the patient. In other words, the objective is to promote a safer outcome for the patient by detecting changes early enough so that an intervention can prevent worsening of the symptoms that could lead to catastrophic outcomes. Hence, patient safety is a key motivation behind clinical surveillance of the patient in the inpatient and even the outpatient, or ambulatory, care setting.

In ECRI's Top 10 Patient Safety Concerns for 2019, several entries bear mentioning as concerns the understanding of how knowledge of a patient's condition can translate into early indications of patient safety. Several of the items highlighted in the table below, and their importance relative to surveillance are paraphrased from the original source [12]:

Item number	Patient safety concern
6	"Failure to detect changes in a patient's condition …across the continuum of care" in which "inadequately trained staff" can fail to respond or rescue a patient in sufficient time.
8	Early detection of sepsis in order to "facilitate timely diagnosis and management" of these patients for the reason of identifying adverse events early and providing the means to treat a patient as soon as possible.
10	Systemic improvements and standardization of patient safety in large and diverse healthcare systems "…to institute structures that effectively allow patient safety priorities … help the organization reduce inconsistencies and embed a strong focus on patient safety."

And, from ECRI's 2019 Top 10 Health Technology Hazards, items 4 and 7 are highlighted in the table below [13]:

Item number	Technology hazard
4	The use of "improperly set ventilator alarm" limit settings can place patients at jeopardy for "hypoxic brain injury or death." Specifically, " … leaks, disconnections, and other failures… can quickly lead to harm if … not identified and rectified promptly [within minutes]." "Healthcare facilities need policies on setting user-adjustable ventilator alarms and protocols…"
7	The setting of customized alarm settings on a per-patient or per condition basis is deemed an important measure for reducing alarm fatigue and hazards associated with nuisance alarms … "improper customization of physiologic monitor alarm settings may result in missed alarms …[and] could prevent staff from learning about significant changes in the patient's physiologic status…" "Failure to recognize and respond to such conditions in a timely manner can result in serious patient injury or death."

Several themes are suggested in each of these items surrounding the following:

■ Failure to recognize and respond to a patient's deteriorating condition.
■ Failure to rectify deterioration promptly.
■ Failure to recognize alarms that may carry clinical import.
■ Organizational focus on reducing inconsistency in treatment or management that carries an impact on patient safety.

Context is, of course, important when it comes to clinical assessment of the patient. This means that as part of the standard clinical procedure of obtaining subjective and objective information on the patient, the assessment and plan associated with treatment should take into account whether the patient presents for, or is at risk for, one or more forms of cardiovascular or respiratory deterioration. Understanding whether and how deterioration is taking place requires clinical training and, so, the intention is not to mislead the reader into thinking that one can simply observe vital signs numbers and make diagnostic conclusions from these alone. The point, though, is that the objective data obtained from the patient through automatically and frequently collected vital signs information serves as an adjunct to help complete the clinical picture of the patient, thereby providing the frontline clinician with an insight into patient state that might not be available under circumstances in which these data are not continuously collected.

Consider example case studies, or scenarios, to illustrate these points, summarized in Table 1.1. Several of these case studies will be referred to subsequently in the text to assist in demonstrating the application of surveillance using vital signs, and, therefore, serve as illuminating examples.

Each of these scenarios provides information key to the overall assessment, planning, and diagnosis from the perspective of clinical surveillance through the signs and symptoms presented and through observations and history (that is, past medical history and history of present illness). Thus, in many cases, the vital signs can provide an indication of an impending deterioration that, if unchecked, can be fatal.

Case 1: a female patient suffered a ground-level fall, is elderly, and is prescribed a blood thinner. The patient has experienced an increasing blood pressure over the course of the past 30 minutes, with a decreasing heart rate and diminished respirations. Increasing blood pressure and the concomitant decrease in pulse and respirations is a concern for a possible intracranial bleed as a result of the fall and exacerbated by blood thinners. The presentation is a concern particularly for the elderly.

Case 2: a male patient has a history of sleep apnea and may be experiencing opioid-induced respiratory depression (OIRD), as indicated by the continuing occurrences of sleep apnea and diminished breathing subsequent to pain medication administration. Identification of these events through detection of decreasing respirations, decreasing oxygen saturation, and increasing end-tidal carbon dioxide provides a clue as to the likelihood that respiratory depression is occurring requiring active clinical intervention.

Case 3: a female patient is being weaned from post-operative mechanical ventilation. This is the process whereby external respiratory support is removed as the patient assumes the work of breathing (WoB) as she recovers from coronary bypass grafting (CABG) surgery. During coronary artery bypass grafting, the patient is administered powerful drugs in the form of analgesics, anesthetics, muscle relaxants, and paralytics that cause the cessation of spontaneous breathing, necessitating external respiratory support. As these drugs are metabolized and excreted, the patient slowly begins to assume the task of breathing on her own again.

Table 1.1 Case Study Scenarios Used as Exemplars of Clinical Surveillance

Case study	Narrative	Key observations and vital signs
1	An 80-year-old, 45 kg woman arrives in the emergency department after having suffered a ground-level fall. Controlled bleeding to the back of the head is noted and the patient is completely alert. The patient is breathing regularly and adequately, and clear and equal bilateral breath sounds are noted based upon auscultation. Patient pulse is regular and strong, but a non-invasive blood pressure (NiBP) measurement increase is noted within the first 60 minutes since the fall: the first NiBP measurement 60 minutes ago was 150/80 mmHg with a pulse of 80 bpm. Breathing at that time was observed to be 20 breaths per minute (br/min) and oxygen saturation was determined to be 98% on room air. Now, blood pressure has risen to 190/95 mmHg, pulse has dropped to 50 bpm, and respirations are now reduced to 12 br/min. The patient is diaphoretic and is expressing 5/10 pain (unchanged, unprovoked, non-radiating) in the occipital area of her skull (injury site). The patient has a history of heart disease and myocardial infarction. The patient has prescriptions for coumadin, nitroglycerin, and baby aspirin. The patient has no known drug allergies and no history of stroke. The patient's left pupil, however, now indicate signs of dilation.	a. Ground-level fall b. Controlled bleeding c. Alert and oriented to person, place, time, and event(s) d. Blood pressure increase e. Pulse decrease f. Respiration decrease g. Blood thinner, nitroglycerin h. Left pupil showing signs of dilation i. Pain level unchanged
2	A 55-year-old, 90 kg man has just completed hip replacement surgery and is convalescing in the medical surgical unit. He is receiving Dilaudid for pain management as required. He has a home continuous positive air pressure (CPAP) machine, and his wife reports that he "snores a lot" as well as the observation that he has experienced many bouts of apnea that "scared her." He is in the hospital because he required hip replacement surgery which is the reason he is convalescing today postoperatively in the medical surgical unit.	a. 55-year-old, 90 kg male b. Postsurgical c. Opioid pain medication (PRN) d. History of apnea, CPAP use e. Changes in respiration (f_R), oxygen saturation (SpO_2), end-tidal carbon dioxide ($etCO_2$)

(Continued)

Table 1.1 (Continued) Case Study Scenarios Used as Exemplars of Clinical Surveillance

Case study	Narrative	Key observations and vital signs
	Overnight, he has experienced bouts of low oxygenation saturation and bradypnea followed by several bouts of apnea. These events are known because he has received continuous capnography monitoring since arriving from the operating room. Continuous monitoring of his vital signs showed a reduction and trend in several measured parameters over time, including oxygen saturation, respiration, and end-tidal carbon dioxide levels. Oxygen saturation is presently hovering at 95% on 3 liters per minute (L/min) of oxygen via nasal cannula. End-tidal carbon dioxide is rising slowly from 35 → 55 mmHg and respiration has been decreasing over the last 30 minutes from 18 br/min to 10 br/min.	f. Respiration (f_R) decrease from 18 br/min → 10 br/min; g. $etCO_2$ rise from 35 mmHg → 55 mmHg in 30 minutes h. Oxygen saturation (SpO_2) of 95% on 3 L/min nasal cannula
3	A 60-year-old, 67 kg woman is recovering post coronary artery bypass grafting (CABG) surgery. She returned from surgery 90 minutes ago and is being supported on mechanical ventilation in a mandatory mechanical ventilator mode at 12 br/min, a positive end-expiratory pressure (PEEP) of 5 cmH_2O, a tidal volume (V_T) of 400 milliliters, and is saturating (SpO_2) at 100% on 60% inspired oxygen fraction (FiO_2). During weaning, and, in particular, at transition from mandatory to spontaneous breathing where she is now breathing at an average rate of 16 br/min and a measured tidal volume of 100 mL, the mechanical ventilator begins to alarm, indicating increased peak pressure and low tidal volume alarm. Patient oxygen saturation on an inspired oxygen fraction of 21% oxygen was 96% and has now declined to 90%.	a. Post-CABG surgery b. Postoperative mechanical ventilation c. Spontaneous breathing at a rate of 16 br/min and tidal volume of 100 mL d. Oxygen saturation on 21% oxygen (room air) is 96% → 90% in 15 minutes e. Low tidal volume and high peak pressure alarms
4	A 65-year-old, 70 kg man presents in the emergency department with shortness of breath (SoB), a non-invasive blood pressure (NiBP) of 90/56 mmHg, oxygen saturation (SpO_2) of 88% on room air, crackles in the lungs (verified through auscultation), and a pulse of 110 bpm. The patient reportedly had not taken his prescribed Furosemide and is now running a fever and is beginning to express signs of atrial fibrillation.	a. 65-year-old, shortness of breath b. Atrial fibrillation c. Decreased blood pressure d. (Low) blood pressure 90/56 mmHg e. Pulse 110 bpm f. Febrile g. Medications: Furosemide

The balance of reducing external ventilatory support while regaining spontaneous support is guided by algorithms and protocols adhered to by the clinical staff. Yet, adverse events can occur along the way. One such adverse event is the occlusion of the endotracheal tubing (ETT) that delivers needed oxygen and removes waste carbon dioxide from the patient. Should the endotracheal tube become clogged or occluded by mucous, air will not be able to be moved into and out of the lungs. As a result, pressure in the tubing will increase and the volume of delivered oxygen will decrease or cease altogether. This will result in alarms associated with high peak pressure and reduced ventilatory volume and rate. The combination of these events is an immediate call to action to intervene.

Case 4: a male patient who is prescribed furosemide to reduce extra bodily fluid is experiencing pulmonary edema likely due to right ventricular heart failure. Furosemide is a powerful diuretic often prescribed for patients with heart, kidney and liver disease to manage fluid retention. When untreated or treated inadequately, this can result in increased fluid volume in the lungs, decreased lung perfusion, and increasing shortness of breath (SoB) while the reduced perfusion translates into reduced (and reducing) hemoglobin oxygen saturation content. Detecting the physical and physiological signs of respiratory distress are key to intervention before the patient lapses into complete respiratory failure.

In each of these cases, the combination of vital signs with observations provides insight into the state of each patient. As we will see in the coming chapters, the use of these data through the application of various mathematical techniques and clinical insights can result in the identification of patient deterioration in earlier stages, promoting earlier intervention.

1.2 The State Vector Analogy

The state of the patient is represented via a series of subjective and objective findings, followed by an assessment that then leads to a plan of action and treatment. The state, therefore, defines the current findings and health of the various subsystems: cardiovascular, respiratory, renal, digestive, and so on. By analogy, the state of the patient is akin to the state of a moving object over time: the position, velocity, and acceleration of an object (say, an automobile or aircraft or spacecraft) is completely defined by this state vector, and it is through this state vector that the past history is known and future state may be projected with a degree of accuracy limited only by the current knowledge of the state and the degree to which the current state had deviated from past projections. The state of the patient, by analogy, is understood by the history of present and past illness, the patient's general state of health guided by the knowledge of anatomy, physiology, chemistry, microbiology, and medicine, and the patient's past response to treatment, as well as the speed with which the current onset of the present illness occurred.

Oftentimes, analogies can suffice to solidify concepts in the mind so that they can be better understood when applied to the original target problem. Although not a perfect analogy, one can think of the state of the person's health in terms of the three-dimensional state of a spacecraft, such as shown in the diagrams of Figure 1.1 (a), depicting a generic spacecraft with the forces acting through its center of mass, or Figure 1.1(b), depicting the undocked Apollo 11 Lunar Module, *Eagle*, with state defined as its position and velocity as well as its internal health and status of its various power, environmental, and control subsystems. The external observations (i.e., the three-dimensional position and velocity vectors), and the internal state (i.e., power, environmental, control systems) directly describe the health and status of the spacecraft.

The overall state of both spacecraft are thus described as the combination of the state of internal health and status (i.e., power, fuel, oxygen) and external health and status (i.e., its position, velocity, acceleration). Hence, the representation of the state of the spacecraft comprises all of these components. The external health and status can be represented as a state vector, $\vec{R}(t)$, expressed mathematically below by Equation 1.1:

$$\vec{R}(t) = \begin{bmatrix} x(t) \\ y(t) \\ z(t) \\ \dot{x}(t) \\ \dot{y}(t) \\ \dot{z}(t) \end{bmatrix} \tag{1.1}$$

The position at time t in three dimensions is given by $x(t)$, $y(t)$, $z(t)$. The velocity, or time-derivative of position, at the same time t in three dimensions is given by $\dot{x}(t), \dot{y}(t), \dot{z}(t)$. Thus, the position and velocity at any desired time point, t^*, is known. Furthermore, the past and future positions

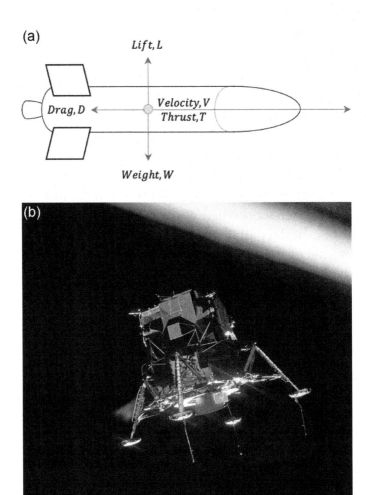

Figure 1.1 (a) Spacecraft showing forces acting through center of mass; (b) Apollo 11 lunar module Eagle after separation from the command/service module in preparation for de-orbit and landing [14]. Image used with permission of the National Aeronautics and Space Administration.

of the spacecraft at any time in the past, $t_{past} < t^*$, or any time in the future, $t_{future} > t^*$, can be known by projecting the current state backward or forward in time in accordance with the spacecraft equations of motion, based on the model of the trajectory obtained from experimental observations derived from physics – just as physicians and researchers have derived models of the human body. Roughly speaking, the equations of motion define the state at any time in the past or any time in the future as follows in a simplified form in Equation 1.2:

$$\vec{R}(t^*) = \begin{bmatrix} x(t^*) \\ y(t^*) \\ z(t^*) \\ \dot{x}(t^*) \\ \dot{y}(t^*) \\ \dot{z}(t^*) \end{bmatrix} = \begin{bmatrix} x(t_0) + \dot{x}(t_0) \times (\Delta t) + \dfrac{\ddot{x}(t_0)}{2} \times (\Delta t)^2 \\ y(t_0) + \dot{y}(t_0) \times (\Delta t) + \dfrac{\ddot{y}(t_0)}{2} \times (\Delta t)^2 \\ z(t_0) + \dot{z}(t_0) \times (\Delta t) + \dfrac{\ddot{z}(t_0)}{2} \times (\Delta t)^2 \\ \dot{x}(t_0) + \ddot{x}(t_0) \times (\Delta t) \\ \dot{y}(t_0) + \ddot{y}(t_0) \times (\Delta t) \\ \dot{z}(t_0) + \ddot{z}(t_0) \times (\Delta t) \end{bmatrix} \tag{1.2}$$

Equation 1.2 states that the future position and velocity are equal to the current position and velocity propagated (or projected) forward in time by the amount $\Delta t = t^* - t_0$, where t_0 is the initial time from which the state is to be propagated forward, and subject to the current velocity and acceleration, where velocity and acceleration are defined in vector form, respectively, by Equation 1.3:

$$\vec{R}(t^*) = \begin{bmatrix} \dot{x}(t_0) + \ddot{x}(t_0) \times (\Delta t) \\ \dot{y}(t_0) + \ddot{y}(t_0) \times (\Delta t) \\ \dot{z}(t_0) + \ddot{z}(t_0) \times (\Delta t) \end{bmatrix} \tag{1.3}$$

The acceleration term in vector form is given by Equation 1.4:

$$\vec{R}(t^*) = \begin{bmatrix} \ddot{x}(t_0) \\ \ddot{y}(t_0) \\ \ddot{z}(t_0) \end{bmatrix} \tag{1.4}$$

While seemingly complex, the equations expressed in Equation 1.2 simply state that the current state, at time $t = t^*$ is simply equal to the state at a previous time, defined as $t = t_0$ plus the current velocity multiplied by time from current time to desired time, represented as $\Delta t = t^* - t_0$, plus the acceleration multiplied by the square of this time (the factor of one-half is included as a constant of integration). Thus, in this way, the state at any desired time, past or future, is determined based upon the current position, velocity, and acceleration. When subject to no other forces external to the spacecraft, the position, velocity, and acceleration are thereby determined for all time. This, again, is a tremendously simplified model for the benefit of the intended readership (it is assumed that the readership is not well-versed in the details of rocket science). Nevertheless, the analogy represents a rough approximation to the steady state of the human being.

Returning to the physiological state of the patient, the "equations of motion" of the various subsystems (e.g., cardiac, respiratory, renal, digestive, lymphatic) defined in the human body are rather different from the equations of motion of a spacecraft (driven by gravitational fields and the thrusting forces of engines). But, from the cardiovascular and respiratory perspective, the laws of physics apply as well as those established through biology and chemistry at the cellular level. For instance, the heart behaves as a pump and circulates both oxygenated and deoxygenated blood through the arteries and veins, respectively, and to the lungs where the exchange of gases takes place (i.e., carbon dioxide and other waste products upon exhalation; oxygen upon inhalation). Interrelationships exist among these various systems through dependencies. For example, the cardiovascular and respiratory systems are keenly interdependent: oxygenation is achieved through the circulation of the blood and supplying oxygen to the cells of the heart and all cells of the body, and ridding the cells of waste products is dependent on the correct functioning of the lungs. These and other biological, chemical, and physical interrelationships establish and define the "state" of the patient at any one moment in time, and the values of key measurements or findings in the patient represent quantitatively the "state vector" at any time, t^*. From the current state and through knowledge of the "physics" and "trajectory" of the various patient systems, a future state that maintains homeostasis can be inferred. Thus, deviations from the normal state, or homeostasis, represents a notable event which, if sufficiently deviant from the normal state, merits intervention.

1.3 The Decompensating Patient

As has been established, a key objective of clinical surveillance is to identify the deteriorating or decompensating patient through the use of data that are continuously collected in real-time from the patient via those sources of data that are principally derived from patient care devices (PCDs), or medical devices, employed in the monitoring and therapy at the point of patient care. The PCDs provide the primary objective source for insight into the patient as, particularly in high-acuity patient settings, data often speak for the patient, for those patients who are unconscious, recuperating from invasive surgical procedures, or heavily sedated and on pain medication.

A particular patient class susceptible to decompensation is the patient recovering from the effects of anesthesia postoperatively and those who are receiving opioid pain medication. One fact of note is that of the 40 million-plus surgeries performed annually in the United States, a significant potential threat to patient safety is adverse respiratory events, such as apnea and respiratory distress leading to respiratory failure [15]. Related to these clinical events are the consequences associated with missing PCD alarm signals from cardiorespiratory monitoring which can provide early indications as to the onset of respiratory distress. Failure to notify clinicians of adverse events in a timely manner can result in injury or even death.

Patients admitted with preexisting respiratory ailments have high mortality rates. Patients in respiratory distress for whom supplemental respiratory support in the form of external mechanical ventilation is required is one key indicator of a patient in significant distress – those at risk for severe illness, injury or death. The frequency of patients requiring emergency mechanical ventilation has been estimated at higher than 44,000 patients per year in the United States alone, with a mortality rate of nearly 40% for patients that develop in-hospital respiratory failure. It also has been estimated that the death rate in patients with respiratory failure is more than twice the estimate for patients experiencing heart attacks, and higher than in those diagnosed with cancer, stroke, or renal failure [15, 16].

The seriousness of respiratory distress surrounding decompensation was exemplified in a study of 92 closed insurance claims (i.e., claims that have been settled) between 1990 and 2009. This study determined that patients who had experienced inadequate postoperative ventilation necessary to support adequate gas exchange (i.e., respiratory depression, or RD) was a significant cause of death and brain damage with as high as 88% of cases estimated to occur within the first day after surgery [17].

Almost all of these cases (97%) were deemed preventable. Forty-two percent (42%) of patients diagnosed with RD were identified within 2 hours, and 16% were identified within 15 minutes, of the last nursing check [17].

These findings are startling and are a call to action. As recently as 2019, the Anesthesia Patient Safety Foundation (APSF) called attention to these and further findings, citing that opioid-induced ventilatory impairment (OIVI) affects as many as 1 in 200 postoperative patients, with 75% of cases occurring within 24 hours of surgery [18, 19].

Opioid-induced respiratory depression (OIRD), RD, and OIVI are often the result of postoperative pain medication depressing pulmonary function, and are a cause of a significant number of emergent intubations, postoperative mortality, and other conditions leading to mortality. Many conditions exacerbate or aggravate respiratory compromise and depression, such as congestive heart failure (CHF), some lung ailments, pulmonary embolism and edema, and airway obstruction [15].

Recommendations from the APSF, the Association for the Advancement of Medical Instrumentation (AAMI), and others advocate for the use of continuous cardiorespiratory monitoring of patients throughout the entire postoperative period to improve surveillance of patients and to ameliorate the risks associated with RD, and, particularly, for those patients at risk for cessation of breathing. Patients diagnosed with or at risk for central or obstructive sleep apnea fall into this category [15].

Respiratory depression, respiratory failure, and determining the need for intervention mandate clinical detection of respiratory inadequacy, such as through measurements, or findings obtained via continuous vital signs monitoring. Examples of key vital signs indicators of respiratory distress include reduced breathing rate and depth, or hypoventilation, non-invasive peripheral oxygen desaturation, and changes in heart rate, or pulse. Measurements such as heart rate, respiration rate, peripheral oxygenation saturation, and blood pressure provide specific data that can indicate the evolution of patient state from stability to instability, including conditions that may result in patient suffering and death [16, 20, 21].

While continuous monitoring of PCD measurements provides real-time and sustained cardio-respiratory data at regular intervals in high-acuity patient environments, other locations around the hospital may lack the ability to collect continuous PCD data. An example of such a location includes the general care unit setting where patient vital signs are monitored less frequently. Yet, the general care unit setting is where many of these decompensation events occur [11]. It is through the measurement of parameters, insight obtained through parameter trended trajectories, and the observed deviation of patient state from normal evolution that it is possible to identify earlier when patients are beginning a downward spiral. This provides the safety net so often absent in general care units that is the norm in intensive care units, emergency departments, and operating rooms. Yet, as many hospitals only employ continuous monitoring in the highest acuity settings, it is, perhaps, time to reevaluate extending continuous monitoring to every location in the hospital setting, on every patient, all the time [11].

The continuous monitoring model can be extended to the home, such as for patients challenged with diabetes, chronic obstructive pulmonary disease

(COPD), or congestive heart failure (CHF). Here, too, patient care device monitoring adds a safety net to detect decompensating patients, particularly those who live alone, so that adverse events and trends can be identified and early interventions can be initiated through timely emergency medical services (EMS) calls.

Examples of physiological consequences in patients experiencing respiratory decompensation include "impaired control of breathing, … impaired airway protection (e.g., inability to swallow or maintain a patent airway), … parenchymal lung disease, … increased airway resistance (i.e., work of breathing, WoB), … hydrostatic pulmonary edema, … [and] right ventricular failure" [15]. Common to the identification and early onset detection in all of these conditions are aspects of physiological monitoring achieved through the use of patient care devices (PCDs). Examples of types of data employed for monitoring of these conditions are categorized and summarized in Table 1.2. Many, if not most, of the parameters listed in Table 1.2 can be captured using various types of medical devices (i.e., physiological monitors, mechanical ventilators) both from within and from outside of the hospital environment.

The various monitoring options suggested in Table 1.2, which abstracts a detailed summary provided in [15], demonstrate some data collection patterns that apply across all types of respiratory decompensation. Data suggested for continuous real-time or periodic collection include:

- Electrocardiogram (ECG)
- Expired carbon dioxide, either through transcutaneous or end-tidal carbon dioxide measurement (P_tCO_2 or $etCO_2$)
- Heart rate or pulse (HR)
- Non-invasive blood pressure (NiBP or NBP)
- Oxygen supplementation through nasal cannula, non-rebreather mask, or bag valve mask (FiO_2)
- Pulse oximetry (SpO_2)
- Respiration rate (RR or f_R)
- Temperature (T)

These data, when taken together with observations and other data obtained *pro re nata* (PRN),* such as serum metabolic panel determination from venous blood draws, imaging, and clinical observation, can be thought of as representing the "state vector" of the patient: the external representation of

---

* Pro re nata for the present circumstances; as needed (Merriam-Webster).

Table 1.2 Types of Objective Data Used to Monitor Cardiac and Respiratory Parameters and Recommended Collection Frequencies [15]

Continuously collected data (i.e., intervals of seconds to minutes)	• Pulse oximetry • Electrocardiogram (ECG) • Transcutaneous carbon dioxide ($PtCO_2$) • End-tidal carbon dioxide ($etCO_2$) • Respiration rate (f_r) • Supplemental oxygen (i.e., delivery method, volume flow rate) • Heart rate (HR) • Non-invasive blood pressure (NiBP)
Frequently collected data (i.e., intervals of several times an hour to several hours)	• Evaluation of level of consciousness and mental status (i.e., alert and oriented to person, place, time, and events) • Evaluation of work of breathing and ability to compensate • Evaluation of lung sounds obtained through auscultation; peripheral and sacral edema • Evaluation of cardiac output; changes in heart electrical activity • Temperature changes
Periodically collected data (i.e., intervals of hours to days, or as required)	• Arterial blood gas (ABG) measurement (i.e., partial pressures of carbon dioxide, oxygen; calculated potential of hydrogen, pH; blood urea nitrogen, BUN; bicarbonate levels) • Blood glucose and lactate levels • Evaluation of patient's ability to swallow • Echocardiography • Tests of cardiac strain and damage (e.g., cardiac stress tests)

the internal function and status of the patient's various systems that provide an outside observer with an understanding of the behavior and functional health of the patient at any moment in time. Thus, the integrated picture of the patient emerges. Publications in recent years corroborate the use of integrated data in improving the overall outcome assessment and outlook of patients indicating that when these data are taken together, earlier detection of events such as respiratory decompensation can be achieved [23–26].

1.4 Medical and Clinical Significance of Real-Time Data

Human beings and other biological creatures comprise multiple interdependent, interoperable, and integrated subsystems. Each of these subsystems is complex and the interdependencies among them result in behaviors that can be elusive to the layperson unless their interrelationships, anatomy, and patient physiology are thoroughly understood. Thus, what appears to be a symptom in one organ may actually have a root cause in another. Numerous examples abound. Yet, several such examples previously cited may serve to illustrate this point now:

■ Congestive heart failure (CHF) results in increases in fluid volume in the extremities and increases in fluid in the lungs, causing respiratory distress, edema, or fluid retention (particularly in legs, feet, sacral area) due to the back-up of fluid in the interstitial spaces as it is not removed effectively because of the heart's inability to effectively work as a pump.

■ Increased blood pressure due to an increase in intracranial pressure associated with cerebral-vascular accidents and events, such as stroke or head trauma, results from arterial bleeding in the brain. In such cases, increasing brain case pressure results in lowering of intracranial blood flow, causing the heart to attempt to compensate by increasing blood pressure to ensure a large enough volume of oxygenated blood continues to flow into the brain. Increasing pressure in the brain combined with the need to maintain a consistent cardiac output can cause compression of the medulla portion of the brain, resulting in decreased respiration and heart rate. Thus, in patients experiencing increased intracranial pressure, an increase in blood pressure combined with a reduction in heart rate (bradycardia) and respiration (bradypnea) can be observed concomitantly. This combination is often referred to as *Cushing's Triad.**

■ Systemic bloodborne infection results in the body's release of white blood cells to fight infection. As a result of this release, arteriole vasodilation occurs to facilitate the movement of white blood cells throughout the vasculature. This vasodilation causes a reduction in blood pressure due to the increase in arteriole diameter. The net effect is hypotension, or lowering of the blood pressure.

■ Decreasing blood glucose levels due, perhaps, to hypoglycemia as a result of diabetes or the overuse or abuse of insulin, can cause blood glucose levels to fall below 70 mg/dL, resulting in an altered level of consciousness, confusion, and combativeness that can imitate a drug overdose, stroke, or alcohol influence, particularly in extreme cases.[†]

---

* *Cushing's Triad*: bradycardia, hypertension, and irregular respiration: signs of increased intracranial pressure; after Harvey Williams Cushing, MD.

[†] *Hypoglycemia*, The Mayo Clinic. https://www.mayoclinic.org/diseases-conditions/hypoglycemia/symptoms-causes/syc-20373685 Accessed 07/31/2020

Many other examples can be cited, of course. The key here is to provide the reader with an understanding by example of how changes in the physiological state can paint a picture of the patient and that specific changes in state can imply underlying conditions that, when taken together with other diagnostic information, define the state of the patient at any time.

The conditions under which interventions are defined for a patient are based clinically on patient presentation, history of past and present illness, and assessments reported from test findings. In the parlance of the clinician, patient assessment is based on the *subjective* reports of the patient, the *objective* data obtained from observation, and unbiased sources, such as physiological measurements, from which an *assessment* can be made by the clinician, enabling the clinician to define a *plan* of action necessary for treatment. There is a four-letter acronym that is often used by clinicians, and this acronym is "SOAP," with definitions as provided in Table 1.3.

The patient's own report of his or her ailment (or reports of family members, bystanders, others) provides a basis for the subjective component of data.

Measurements obtained from bedside PCDs, imaging, comprehensive metabolic panels, and other forms of measurement fall into the "Objective" category. Measurements are compared with "normal" ranges as well as deviations from those normal ranges in comparison with the patient baseline measurements to evaluate whether observed deviations are significant.

Assessment is the process of putting the pieces together—both subjective and objective—and then creating a plan to treat the patient.

The individual PCD measurements, however, when taken outside of context, can result in an incomplete or inaccurate view of patient state. For example, in the case of a pulse oximeter that measures heart rate (pulse)

Table 1.3 Clinical Assessment Using the SOAP Methodology

Components of SOAP	Definitions
Subjective	What the patient tells you (i.e., history of present and past illness)
Objective	What is observed from the data (i.e., clinician observations of the patient, vital signs)
Assessment	What the objective and subjective information tells you about the underlying cause and the likely differential diagnosis of the patient
Plan	What treatment options are appropriate based on the assessment

and peripheral oxygen saturation, a frequently used measure for patient arterial oxygen saturation inadequacy is a pulse oximetry reading at or below a specific fixed threshold limit value (say, 90%). Parameter threshold limits that define an actionable level of change in a given parameter vary by clinical significance, protocols, and health systems, as well as by clinical preferences. Taken by itself, an oxygen saturation reading may or may not indicate true desaturation in the patient if a measurement or even a series of measurements drops below the value of 90%. Why? For any one or more of the following reasons:

- Patient agitation leading to incorrect or unstable measurements obtained through pulse oximetry.
- Poor or low measurements resulting from cold patient fingers, poor perfusion or postoperative chill, or fingernail polish or other types of opaque obstructions.
- Poor or mis-calibrated pulse oximetry sensors.
- Physiological monitoring equipment failure.
- Incorrect placement of pulse oximetry finger sensors.
- Blood pressure cuff occlusions due to blood pressure cuffs being placed on the same arm as the pulse oximetry sensor.
- Patient movement or intentional dislodgement of the pulse oximetry sensor.
- Other causes that may relate to patient, PCD, environment, or care provider.

The challenge, therefore, in obtaining accurate measurements is that the sources of aberrations that affect the accuracy and reliability of the measurements can be obscured, and the equipment cannot detect or discriminate between true measurements and false or aberrant measurements as limited by the measurement capability of the equipment and the inability to automate an understanding of the context surrounding the patient. In other words, the PCD that is performing the measurement lacks the context of whether the source of the measurement, or the measurement itself, can be trusted. Thus, if and when a measurement deviates from a predefined range of acceptable single parameter measurement values (i.e., value breaches a threshold), then an alarm or notification will be annunciated. Yet, threshold breaches based on single measurement values can, for the aforementioned reasons, occur quite frequently. If alarm signals are generated and transmitted on the basis of these single parameter threshold breaches, then the result will be alarm signals with many (perhaps most) not carrying any clinically actionable information or value: clinical staff will be caused to react to noise in which most of the events exceeding thresholds are non-actionable from a medical or clinical perspective. That is, the alarm signals do not carry information germane to whether impending danger to the patient is imminent requiring immediate intervention. Hence, the alarm signals that are designed to annunciate in order to notify clinicians of emergent events can falsely inform the clinician, often repeatedly, leading to secondary and tertiary effects that can and do impact patient care. Examples of secondary or tertiary effects include inducing fatigue in the clinicians, resulting in their failing to interpret an actual event as real. Such a failure to recognize an actual event that carries clinical import is referred to as a false negative (FN) event [27].

Carrying this point further, if a clinician is notified over and over that a patient has a low oxygen saturation reading, for example, then the clinician may become indifferent to the alarm signal events to the point that he or she will disregard the alarm signal annunciations. The effect can be taken to the extreme, in which an alarm signal may actually be true, but the clinician can become conditioned to ignore it based on the large quantity of past alarm signals that were found to be clinically non-actionable (that is, carried no clinically significant meaning). The effect can be disastrous—to the point that a patient is harmed or killed—based on ignoring a true event [27].

Thus, the purpose of clinical surveillance is twofold: (1) provide the earliest of notifications regarding patient decompensation or decline, while (2) reducing the number or quantity of false alarms communicated to the care provider that minimize or negate false negative events. The challenge is how to communicate only the essential, clinically actionable information while suppressing the non-clinically actionable information. Accomplishing this balance is an art, as the measurements used to identify significant clinical events do not always carry complete or correct information. This fact has led to what has been published in recent years as the concept of "alarm fatigue" [28]: excessive communications of alarm notifications associated with medical devices based on measurement threshold breaches. Most alarm signals generated using signal threshold breaches have been shown to be almost entirely non-clinically actionable (as will be discussed later). Hence, the potential to notify clinicians incorrectly that there is an actionable event occurring with a patient can and does result in inefficiency, time and effort waste, and physical and mental fatigue on the part of the clinician—fatigue that can indeed result in the possibility of patient harm due to the fact that the provider is distracted or ignores the continuing or repeated annunciations of non-actionable alarms and notifications. Approaches to ameliorating alarm signals have been reported for years, and many techniques have been suggested, ranging from imposing delays on the annunciation of an alarm to changing the threshold values to be less sensitive.

The AAMI has conducted and reported on the patient safety impact of medical device alarms—both audible and remotely communicated—for years, and though there has been a significant amount of research into techniques for alarm signal reduction, there is no one approach that works perfectly for all patients, all units or wards, and all situations [29]. Thus, although simple alarms can be communicated as threshold breaches associated with the value of a particular finding exceeding a known parameter threshold, the impact of the parameter from the perspective of whether it is clinically actionable is unknown unless more information and greater context is brought to bear relative to the situation and the patient. A good example of this is the setting of limit thresholds on the peripheral oxygen saturation parameter, SpO_2. The finding SpO_2 is a proxy measurement for the arterial oxygen content associated with the amount of oxygen contained in the hemoglobin found in red blood cells. Values of oxygen saturation range from 0–100%, with values of 95% and above typically accepted as normal (i.e., not requiring supplemental oxygen or other interventions).

As the value of SpO_2 declines below limit thresholds defined as clinically significant, PCDs measuring this parameter are often set to annunciate an alarm. These alarms are communicated to clinical staff to respond to the event as requiring an intervention. In most cases, however, the alarms that are annunciated are not clinically actionable—some studies have shown that these alarms are almost entirely non-actionable. In clinical settings such as intensive care units, in which the average number of alarms per patient per day can range on the order of 350, and upwards of 87% of alarm signals can be deemed clinically non-actionable, it is easy to understand how alarm signals (or more, depending on the study reported) can become overwhelming, and that the use of different approaches, including multi-parameter alarm signal methodologies to reduce frequent false alarms, will be necessary to sort the true, clinically-actionable alarm signal from the false alarm signal [30, 31, 56].

1.5 Chapter Summary

This chapter introduces the reader to the concept of clinical surveillance, how it is defined, and how measurements obtained from PCDs can be used to assist in surveilling the patient, and which types of parameters are informative regarding cardiorespiratory monitoring of the patient. The chapters that follow address the type of data normally collected using PCDs and how these data can be employed and integrated through clinical practice to aim for increased effectiveness of alarm notifications while reducing the overall false positive alarm burden related to non-actionable alarm signals. The approaches and techniques to clinical surveillance presented here are empirical in nature and can vary by protocol, health system, department, and clinical unit. Yet, it is the author's objective that by exposing the reader to these various techniques, the reader will develop an understanding of the benefits of clinical surveillance and how a specific mathematical methodology can be employed and tailored to meet the requirements of a particular clinical setting.

Chapter 2

Use of Patient Care Device Data for Clinical Surveillance

2.1 Patient Care Device (PCD) Integration

Patient vital signs monitoring involves closely observing the patient's physiological states over time, as was discussed in Chapter 1. Yet, maintaining close and continuous observation of patients can be daunting: to do so requires a sharp eye by a clinician (physician, nurse, respiratory therapist) and can be exhausting work, particularly when considering that the ratio of patients to nurses can average five-to-one or more outside of the intensive care unit setting [32]. Surveilling half-a-dozen patients can be difficult and tedious work.

Patient vital signs monitoring, in general, involves measuring physiological parameters typically associated with cardiac and respiratory function, although other subsystem monitoring (e.g., brain, endocrine, etc.) does take place, as well as the monitoring of patient fluid and food intake and outputs (i.e., outputs in the form of blood, urine, and fecal matter). Physical observations and blood chemistry assessments obtained from serum blood draws including measurement of key ions, and blood chemistry occur regularly, based on the orders of the attending physician.

Some examples of vital signs measurements include (but are not limited to):

- Heart rate (HR; in units of beats per minute, bpm)
- Blood pressure (systolic and diastolic; in units of millimeters of mercury—mmHg)

■ Respiration (breath rate or frequency, f_R; in units of breaths per minute, br/min, or respirations per minute, rpm)
■ Peripheral oxygen saturation (SpO_2; in units of %)
■ Temperature (T; in units of Celsius)
■ Expired carbon dioxide ($etCO_2$; in units of millimeters of mercury—mmHg)
■ Tidal volume, or expired breath volume (Vt; in units of milliliters per breath—mL)
■ Peak inspiratory pressure, or the pressure associated with inspiratory effort required of an external mechanical ventilator, in intubated patients (PIP; in units of centimeters of water—cmH_2O)
■ Positive end-expiratory pressure (PEEP; in units of centimeters of water—cmH_2O)
■ ECG (electrocardiogram; "3-lead" and "12-lead" measurements, for example)

Some examples of metabolic information obtained from serum blood draws associated with comprehensive metabolic panels include (but are not limited to):

■ pH (potential of hydrogen)
■ $PaCO_2$ (partial pressure of carbon dioxide; in units of *millimeters of mercury, mmHg*)
■ PaO_2 (partial pressure of oxygen; in units of *millimeters of mercury, mmHg*)
■ HCO_3^- (bicarbonate; in units of *millimoles per liter, mmol or mEq*)
■ Na^+ (sodium ions; in units of *millimoles per liter, mmol or mEq*)
■ K^+ (potassium ions; in units of *millimoles per liter, mmol or mEq*)
■ Cl^- (chlorine ions; in units of *millimoles per liter, mmol or mEq*)
■ BUN (blood urea nitrogen; in units of *milligrams per deciliter*)
■ Cr (creatinine; in units of *milligrams per deciliter*)
■ Glu (glucose; in units of *milligrams per deciliter*)
■ AG ($AG = Na^+ + K^+ - Cl^- - CO_2$; computed both with and without albumen correction) [33]

Some examples of observations and assessments performed by the clinician or observed by the clinician:

■ Skin color, tone, clamminess, diaphoresis
■ Pupil dilation, equality, responsiveness (e.g., pupils equal, round, and reactive to light)

■ Lung sounds via auscultation (e.g., lungs clear and equal bilaterally; lung sounds can include rhonchi, rales, wheezing)
■ Fluid balance (fluid intake in the form of oral, intravenous; fluid output in the form of blood, urine, feces)
■ Pain quality and severity assessment (subjective assessment on a numeric scale of 0–10, with 10 being the worst pain, or faces scale—typically used with pediatric or non-vocal patients)
■ Patient conscious awareness (to self, place or surroundings, time, events)
■ Last oral intake (last food or water consumed)

Some examples of imaging and radiographic sources of data:

■ MR (magnetic resonance imaging)
■ CT (computed tomography)
■ XR (X-Ray)
■ US (ultrasound)

Of these groups of findings, the vital signs, metabolic, and radiographic contributions represent principally objective information (i.e., least susceptible to subjective interpretation). Yet, metabolic and radiographic information are not continuous sources of data. A set of findings obtained from a Comprehensive Metabolic Panel (CMP) may occur several times per day (e.g., in the case of an ICU patient being managed on mechanical ventilation), and can consist of blood serum analyses or analyses of other bodily fluids (e.g., urine, feces, and various cultures). Comprehensive metabolic panels provide important information regarding pH balance and metabolism, as referred to in Table 2.1. Yet, findings from comprehensive metabolic panels are not collected as frequently as vital signs measurements from PCDs.

Thus, if one is looking for real-time information on a patient, vital signs provide the best objective source of frequently-collected objective information, together with direct observation of the patient. Of course, changes in vital signs may trigger the need for other findings, such as radiographic and blood chemistry assessments. Continuous monitoring of vital signs at regular intervals of one minute or more frequently can catch key changes in patient condition that can signal emergent events on a patient. Data collection gaps of even 30 minutes can result in tragedy in which individuals die because of missed information germane to the evolving state of the patient [34–36]. Unfortunate tragedies can carry with them valuable lessons to reduce the likelihood of future adverse events. A key lesson that has evolved over the years is that surveillance through frequent or continuous

Table 2.1 Example of Substances Measured and Reported on in a Comprehensive Metabolic Panel

Substance	Unit of measure	Normal range	Definition
Albumin	g/dL	3.4–5.4	Protein created in the liver; most abundant protein found in blood plasma; maintains oncotic pressure in arteries; transports hormones and fatty acids
Alkaline phosphatase	IU/L	20–130	Concentrated principally in liver and bile ducts, kidney, bone, and intestinal mucosa, and plays an important role in intestinal homeostasis
Alanine aminotransferase (ALT)	IU/L	4–36	Enzyme most commonly found in the liver. Taken together with AST (below), provides a measurement of general liver health
Aspartate aminotransferase (AST)	IU/L	8–33	Catalyzes and supports enzyme and amino acid metabolism
Blood urea nitrogen (BUN)	mg/dL	6–20	Waste product removed by kidneys as a result of the metabolism of protein
Calcium (Ca^+)	mg/dL	8.5–10.2	Electrolyte supporting heart, muscles, and nerves
Chloride (Cl^-)	Mmol/L	96–106	Electrolyte supporting fluid balance and pH balance
Carbon dioxide	Mmol/L	23–29	Waste product from respiration and metabolism at the cellular level
Creatinine (Cr)	mg/dL	0.6–1.1 (F) 0.7–1.3 (M)	Results from the breakdown of creatine phosphate in the muscles; waste product excreted by kidneys
Glucose	mg/dL	70–100	Primary source of cellular energy supporting metabolism
Potassium (K^+)	mEq/L	3.7–5.2	Electrolyte supporting fluid balance and pH balance
Sodium (Na^+)	mEq/L	135–145	Electrolyte supporting fluid balance and pH balance and nerves
Total bilirubin	mg/dL	0.1–1.2	Waste product of liver
Total protein	g/dL	6.0–8.3	Total protein content in blood

Note: IU/L = international units per liter.

Source: https://medlineplus.gov/ency/article/003468.htm

vital signs monitoring can be achieved using PCDs in which data are collected from the bedside, processed, and communicated to providers so that action can be taken to intervene before irreversible adverse events occur. Collecting data from PCDs is, therefore, an essential function in terms of patient safety. The data collection process is often referred to as medical device integration (MDI) or PCD integration (PCDI), and a treatment of this subject has been covered by the author in earlier texts. A brief overview of MDI is covered in the following section to aid the reader unfamiliar with the subject.

2.2 Patient Care Device Data Integration

The process of collecting data from PCDs for the dual purposes of charting and surveillance is found within the realm of medical device integration (MDI). The logistics and technological details of implementing MDI within a hospital environment are detailed here and in several references [1, 2, 8, 38, 39].

The process of collecting and transmitting data from medical devices typically involves communicating data through patient care device connectivity over a local area network (LAN), which is possible with those medical devices that support such communication, or using a serial-to-network translation device (often referred to as a "bridge"), similar to those shown in Figure 2.1 and Figure 2.2.

The physical and logical connectivity and communication of data from medical devices in general, particularly with physiological monitoring such as found in intensive care units (ICUs), has become more standardized from the perspective that most physiological monitoring and bedside therapeutic technology communicates through a common standard to electronic health record systems utilizing some form of the Health Level Seven (HL7®) Standard [http://www.hl7.org]. Yet, communication of all types and varieties of data, from cardiac and respiratory waveforms to integration of discrete data from ancillary devices such as mechanical ventilators and other therapeutic equipment at the bedside still has a long way go. Some medical devices, such as the aforementioned physiological monitors, communicate over LANs, either through hardwiring or wireless communication (i.e., via 802.11 a/b/g, or n protocols). Other medical devices only communicate via serial ports. Whether communicating over LAN or serial port, there currently is no manufacturing mandate that dictates to which specific physical and

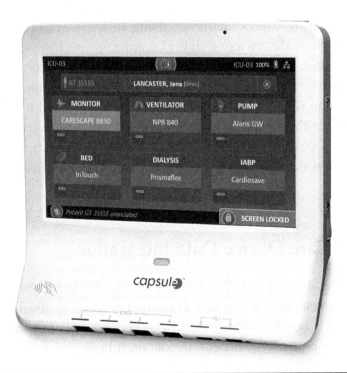

Figure 2.1   Neuron. Courtesy of Capsule Technologies. Used with permission.

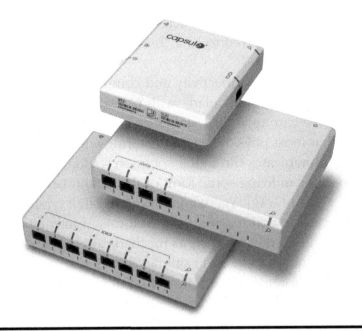

Figure 2.2   Axon. Courtesy of Capsule Technologies. Used with permission.

logical communications protocols medical devices must adhere. Furthermore, while discrete data are oftentimes readily communicated (i.e., individual heart rate, respiration rate, pulse oximetry measurements), waveforms, historically, such as electrocardiograms, plethysmography, capnography, and pressure-volume traces from many mechanical ventilators still follow unique vendor-specific norms. The ubiquity of MDI has improved greatly through the efforts of such organizations as HL7®, IHE International and through IHE PCD initiatives surrounding waveform, alarm, and PCD data collection efforts at creating nominal messaging transactions [39].

Over the years, the technology surrounding generalized data collection from PCDs has advanced to the point that point-of-care communication from medical devices follows many standards and profiles, such as Health Level Seven® (HL7) and the IHE PCD profiles outlined above. In addition, the use of both wired and wireless connectivity has advanced to better facilitate clinical workflow in and around the healthcare enterprise for PCD data collection. It should be remembered that the benefit of automating the collection of patient care device data is not solely in having access to the data, but also in making those data available for downstream processing and for access by frontline clinicians. Hence, emphasis on facilitating access to data to improve clinical workflow, visualization and notifications of evolving states of the collected data are important tools for clinician diagnostic and patient care management tasks.

Several published standards, such as the Institute of Electrical and Electronics Engineering (IEEE) 11073 standards, HL7® standards, and the IHE International PCD profiles detail the semantics and messaging formats of these PCD communications, and is outside of the scope of the focus of this text. It is, however, worthwhile to point out the three IHE International medical device communication profiles, in particular, that the three specific profiles related to medical device communication including the Device Enterprise Communication (DEC), Alert Communication Management (ACM), and Waveform Content Module (WCM) profiles are based on the aforementioned HL7® standards [39]. These communication profiles enable communication interoperability with electronic health record (EHR) systems and applications that support patient care. Per the IHE Wiki website,* the definitions in Table 2.2 apply.

The methods of PCD data communication are very much within the purview and control of the medical device manufacturer. While many manufacturers have evolved toward more standardized modes of communication

---

* https://wiki.ihe.net/index.php/Patient_Care_Device

Table 2.2   IHE International Profile Definitions [40]

Profile	IHE definition
ACM	"Alert Communication Management [ACM] enables the remote communication of point-of-care medical device alert conditions ensuring the right alert with the right priority to the right individuals with the right content (e.g., evidentiary data). It also supports alarm escalation or confirmation based on dissemination status, such as whether the intended clinician has received and acknowledged the condition."
DEC	"Device Enterprise Communication [DEC] supports publication of information acquired from point-of-care medical devices to applications such as clinical information systems and electronic health record systems, using a consistent messaging format and device semantic content."
WCM	"Waveform Communication Management [WCM] will extend the [DEC] profile to provide a method for passing near real-time waveform data using HL7 v2 observation messages. For example, passing wave snippets as evidentiary data in an alarm message communicated using [ACM] transactions."

(as detailed above), there is, as of today, no specific or singular method or industry conformance requirement that is mandated as part of a general manufacturing standard for communication. Ergo, some manufacturers have employed their own proprietary mechanisms for medical device data export from their PCDs. There certainly are financial and workflow motivations to provide straightforward mechanisms to integrate PCD data: healthcare systems today (most of which the author is familiar) expect medical devices to be able to integrate their data into the deployed electronic health record systems. Hence, the business motivation for communicating seamlessly and in accordance with current standards and profiles exists. But the fact that so many legacy PCDs remain in use within the healthcare enterprise necessitates third-party integrators and the use of MDI platforms to facilitate communicating PCD data from both legacy and more contemporary medical devices to support clinical monitoring, assessments, surveillance, and the documentation requirements of clinicians as well as the integration of PCD data from multiple sources to support clinical surveillance.

Because the mechanics of PCD data export communication can vary (i.e., LAN versus serial port), PCD "intermediaries," or platforms, that can translate and transform data from their more vendor-proprietary formats and data communications export mechanisms into more universal formats have emerged. Companies that provide this intermediary type of function have arisen over the years. The intermediary function is often referred to as "middleware" as it operates in the space between the PCD and the electronic health record system (EHR). This intermediary function can comprise both hardware and software to facilitate such communication, as illustrated by the platform hardware depicted in Figure 2.1 and Figure 2.2. These hardware are examples of platforms, together with their accompanying server and device translation software, which support translation from serial connectivity from a wide variety of PCDs to LAN, and facilitate transformation of vendor-proprietary data formats into the HL7® and IHE messaging formats previously described.

The MDI middleware performs the translation function from the vendor-specific, proprietary data communication formats (i.e., both physical mechanism and data or semantic communication formats) into more usable formats consistent with the needs of end-point data capture systems, such as the aforementioned EHR systems. The hardware and software query for data from the PCDs by connecting with them using the proprietary physical mechanism required for the particular PCD (e.g., an Ethernet or serial port), and communicating using the vendor-specific protocols outlined by the PCD manufacturer, as determined through formal published specifications provided by those manufacturers.

The data received from the PCDs is then communicated through a more standardized physical connection (e.g., LAN) on the enterprise network and translated into a semantic messaging format consistent with HL7® and IHE International profiles discussed previously. These latter formats make the data consumable to a wide variety of applications.

The hardware appliances that communicate with the PCDs could range from a computer that provides serial port communication, through a universal serial bus interconnection, or via a proprietary, vendor-specific appliance or device used for this dedicated purpose, as shown in Figure 2.1 or Figure 2.2 The specific approaches are unique to the patient care device middleware vendor [1].

Integrating medical device data into downstream applications such as EHR systems was at one time an esoteric need, of primary interest only to those conducting research in the healthcare environment. Over the course of the past decade, and in part due to the focus on patient safety and meaningful use (MU) guidelines, PCD data integration and interoperability has become a significant part of mainstream healthcare information technology (HIT) system deployment and a key requirement. As of the 2012 U.S. Medical Device Integration (MDI) Study, it was estimated that 40% of U.S. hospitals cite quality improvement as a principal motivation. [40]

Furthermore, studies have estimated that MDI has saved anywhere from 4 to 36 minutes of nursing time and prevented up to 24 data entry errors daily. The cumulative estimate is that MDI can save more than 100 hours of nursing documentation time per day in a typical hospital. [41]

The nursing time saved measure that has been cited as an estimate of efficiency in comparison with manual charting. The time required to manually collect and chart data derived from medical devices is not insignificant, where time estimates of minutes per measurement are not uncommon in the enterprise high-acuity settings of critical care, anesthesia, and other care units, in which regular charting of findings derived from medical devices is required per the plan of care and practice of medicine [41, pp. 4]. Hence, the value of connecting PCDs to the IT infrastructure has been recognized institutionally. Yet, the overall value of MDI exceeds the mechanical task of charting findings in the EHR system.

The interoperability of medical devices refers to the ability of these PCDs to interact with one another to achieve some clinical purpose, in addition to the benefits derived from charting the data automatically. The Association for the Advancement of Medical Instrumentation (AAMI) offers the following definition of interoperability in the context of medical devices [43, pp. 6]:

> [The] ability of medical devices, clinical systems, or their components to communicate in order to safely fulfill an intended purpose.

In the context discussed here, the terms interoperability and integration are used synonymously. The integration of PCD data will refer, for the purpose of this text, to the extraction, translation, and conditioning of these data for use either within a healthcare information technology system, such as an EHR system, or for use as an adjunct for clinical decision support as raw data or as processed events (e.g., alarm signals, trending, or calculations to support clinical assessment and decision making).

While the implementation of hardware and software to achieve the integration of PCDs is an essential element in clinical surveillance, this text is not focused on the treatment related to the capture and conditioning aspects of PCD data—such as medical device drivers, data semantics, and messaging formats. One source that provides a treatment of the technical detail (including software) as examples of such has been developed by the author and is included as a reference [2, pp. 235–75].

2.3 Future Vision of Data for Clinical Surveillance

The value of PCD integration has been estimated to be in the billions of dollars [43]. Integrating PCD data into HIT systems was at one time an esoteric need, of primary interest only to those conducting research in the healthcare environment.

While the usual purpose of MDI is to communicate discrete data from medical devices normally employed as part of the workflow at the point of care (POC) to the EHR system, this use is not the only one, or not even the most interesting use of data from PCDs at the POC. MDI helps to remove the manual and error-prone aspects of recording medical device data: introduction of error due to misinterpretation, errors due to transcription, and errors due to associating information from one patient with that of another. So, from the patient safety perspective, MDI aids in ensuring that data are collected regularly and more accurately on any given patient and that they are communicated reliably to the end-point EHR system. Hence, the availability of rich and timely data derived from medical devices helps to improve the knowledge of the patient state, thereby facilitating better clinical decision-making.

This statement seems to be logical. But what evidence exists to support the assertion that MDI benefits patient care?

The Medical Device Interoperability Coordinating Council (MDICC) and the Westhealth™ Institute published an assessment in March 2013 ("The Value of Medical Device Interoperability") in which they asserted that the intrinsic value in MDI can liberate US$30B+ in annual healthcare savings, principally drawn from improvements in patient safety [43]. As of the publication of that document in 2013 it was estimated that the continuing use and further adoption of the integration of patient care devices was expected "to continue to accelerate … as more than half of U.S. hospitals plan to purchase new MDI solutions" [44].

The value of patient care device integration has received more publicity and a higher profile over the course of the past ten years as the recognition of objective data from patients has been seen as key to supporting more effective patient care management. In 2012, the US Food and Drug Administration (FDA) and AAMI convened a joint summit focused on seeking industry input as part of a "multidisciplinary 'learning event'" aimed at identifying and prioritizing issues in MDI [42, p. 3]. But, why patient care devices and why integrate them now? One reason is the availability of technology that enables access to these types of data:

The advancement and availability of new technologies, coupled with a growing number of serious public health concerns and adverse patient events in which interoperability issues have been [at] root cause.

Furthermore:

Many events, publications, and conversations have focused on the information side of what technology can do. Little attention to date has been focused on the device side of that connectivity, especially as it relates to patient safety. [42, p. 3]

Other uses for data derived through MDI are related to clinical decision-making:

[D]ata need to support clinical decision-making, patient safety, and patient care:

- Rich, timely data for patient care management;
- Temporally and semantically synchronized data to ensure accuracy in patient management;
- Secure, ubiquitous access to ensure availability to data for patient care management. [40, p. 41]

Distilling the key reasons to the following, PCD integration supports very pragmatic and real needs to improve patient care and patient safety, including:

- Reducing clinical documentation transcription errors.
- Improving data accuracy and density within the clinical records.
- Ensuring the complete capture of clinical information on patients and in homogeneity of data.

2.4 Semantic Data Alignment

Once data are obtained from PCDs, they are translated into a common format (e.g., HL7®) and transmitted to the EHR system. This section investigates two key aspects of data integration to EHR systems: the semantic and temporal alignment of data, or synchronization, to ensure their proper posting into the EHR at the appropriate time.

Semantic alignment or synchronization refers to the consistent definition and naming of the data—to ensure that data that are transmitted is correctly interpreted from the perspective of its meaning and then used correctly based upon this meaning. More specifically, semantic alignment seeks to ensure the unambiguous definition of the data and associated units of measure (UOM) of data so that any clinician reviewing these data will have a clear understanding as to its naming, meaning, validity, and timing.

Temporal alignment refers to the accurate and timely association of the collected measurements so that they are aligned with a common time of collection and with each other and communicated to the EHR system with this time of collection. For example, if a measurement of heart rate is obtained from another PCD, and a respiration measurement is obtained from another device, both the time stamp of the heart rate and respiration rate measurement are aligned with respect to a common global time so that the measurements can be understood contextually with respect to one another (e.g.: heart rate of 60 beats per minute and respiration rate of 12 breaths per minute obtained at time 082230).

The AAMI published in their proceedings from the 2012 conference on "MDI: A Safer Path Forward," the four dimensions of interoperability [42, pp. 14–15]:

■ **Data Interoperability:** Agreement/consistency in formatting, storage, querying, and synchronization of data [from patient care devices].
■ **Communication Interoperability:** Consistency in transmission and reception of messages between modes.
■ **Semantic Interoperability:** Agreement/consistency between systems on the meaning of communicated information.
■ **Workflow Interoperability:** Agreement/consistency on how technology supports/shapes the workflow, such as processing or sequencing tasks between participants according to a set of procedural rules; formatting or displaying information and user interfaces.

Others [45] have published similar definitions. From the perspective of practical implementation of PCDI systems, all of these dimensions of interoperability are important and can and do impact the clinical environment from the perspectives of patient safety, efficiency, and clinician effort. Ultimately, interoperability impact overall health system cost. Specific examples:

■ **Incorrectly associating medical device data measured on one patient with another patient.** Associating parameters from a medical device with the wrong patient or incorrectly identifying these data in the clinical record can amount to misinforming the clinical end user. Best case, this can be an irritation to the clinical user and result in delays in terms of requiring recollection of measurements. In a worst-case scenario, the parameter values could be misinterpreted or present a false appearance for clinical decision-making, resulting in a delayed decision or a decision being made in error. For instance, heart rate measured on one patient reported in the chart of another patient is a possible scenario and the consequences, if not investigated, can be disastrous.

■ **Failing to display a measurement in the patient chart.** This scenario involves retrieving the correct parameter from the PCD but failing to populate the value in the patient chart. This can occur if (i) the parameter is not correctly mapped into the EHR system (that is, not mapped as a discrete parameter); (ii) syntax errors exist that cause the measured value to be rejected by the EHR system; or (iii) the parameter is mis-associated with the patient, as described in the preceding bullet point.

■ **Failing to report the correct units of measure on a medical device parameter.** A parameter may be mapped correctly into the EHR system, but the UOM reported from the medical device does not match with the UOM reported within the EHR system. This issue can be minimized if the EHR system takes the UOM from the medical device and reports that directly within the EHR system. However, some EHR systems may require that the UOM be pre-mapped into the clinical chart and does not use the UOM as reported from the medical device. The impact here is seemingly obvious: reporting a measurement with units of liters instead of milliliters, or centimeters of water versus millimeters of Mercury, is significant. In many cases this will be obvious to the clinical end user. But, for the fatigued or distracted clinician, this simply adds more burden and the possibility of making an error.

■ **Using medical device data that contain incorrect time stamps.** Incorrect timing or errors in the time associated with measurements from a medical device (e.g., blood pressure taken at 10:00 is stamped as 10:02) can have an adverse clinical impact in terms of patient safety, therapy, and/or treatment. Stale data, or incorrectly time-stamped data, can have deleterious impacts particularly if medication administrations are dependent on the timing.

When the measurement of parameters is associated with clinical decision-making, the impact can be acute, for instance, when the administration of a drug is dependent upon the value of a measurement (e.g., blood pressure measurement and the administration of a vasodilator). Alternately, measurement of medical device parameters, such as blood pressure or pulse measurement, and administration of anesthetics during surgery, where anesthesiologists are using the measured values to determine the administration of dosing, can have profound effects on patient care management. There are also technical and record-keeping implications associated with errors in measurement time recording: the time stamps of the medical device parameters are recorded in the patient chart based upon the time stamp associated with the data received from the medical device. The concern is the use of a time stamp taken from the medical device itself wherein the medical device time is not synchronized with a common or accepted universal time clock. Many medical devices in service today cannot synchronize their internal clocks with a common or external time source. As a result, their internal clocks tend to drift over time. If not maintained regularly, the internal medical device clocks can deviate appreciably from the network or universal time. Clinical or biomedical engineering personnel typically will need to resynchronize medical device clocks at a regular intervals. This serves to reduce the impact of medical device time deviation but will not eliminate it. The best approach, aside from medical devices that can synchronize automatically with a universal time source, is to employ time stamps from an external clock via the use of an MDI platform. The MDI platform should be able to assign time stamps to medical device data so that these are synchronized with the network time or universal time. For example, time stamps synchronized with a source such as the National Institute of Standards and Technology (NIST).

- **Errors caused by differences in the interpretation of measurements obtained from different medical devices.** Errors in associating measurement values from one medical device with those of another that perform similar functions can also have negative clinical impacts. A key example is the mechanical ventilator: different manufacturers may employ somewhat varying definitions, or may offer modes of operation that are not universally understood or employed by other manufacturers. The result is that one manufacturer's medical device may have a unique set of parameter mappings, and these may not map 1:1 to another manufacturer's device that supports the same clinical function in the same care unit. As a result, it is necessary to develop different device parameter mappings, or only to include a subset of mappings that convey the same information across both (or multiple) manufacturers. The net effect can be a reduced representation of the overall data required by the affected clinicians and, thereby, add to their workflow by requiring that the unmapped fields be collected and entered manually. This can have the effect of defeating the overall purpose and benefit of automated PCDI, adding to the workflow burden, and increase the likelihood of data entry errors, misinterpretation of data, and poor alignment of data in terms of timing within the EHR.

For example, an EHR may have a patient chart tailored for a specific type of mechanical ventilator, in which all of the parameters are recorded and the clinical staff is familiar with the expected data and the location in which they are to appear in the patient chart. Should a different mechanical ventilator be employed, however, that performs the same clinical function (e.g., a second brand of equivalent mechanical ventilator), and the parameters do not post into the chart properly, are missing, or have different UOMs, then this can impact workflow. The misinterpretation of the parameter values can result in patient safety hazards and in lost staff time associated with correcting parameter values, as well as requiring a remapping of the parameter values within the EHR system.

Now that the importance of capturing aligned, clearly delineated data from PCDs has been established, it is time now to turn to the use of multiple data elements from several sources and their utility in clinical decision-making.

2.5 Combining Data from Multiple Sources for Clinical Surveillance

The diagram of Figure 2.3 illustrates the concept of multiple sources of data available on a single patient:

■ Patient care devices (including point-of-care and medical imaging);
■ Clinical observations; and,
■ Serum or laboratory metabolic panels and pathology.

Patient Care Devices   Observations

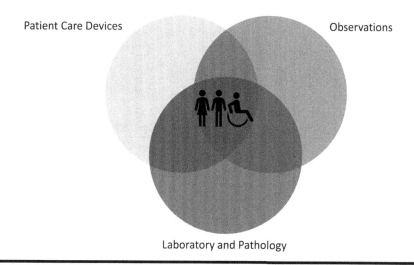

Laboratory and Pathology

Figure 2.3   Various classes of data used to describe the state of the patient and for diagnostic purposes. The categories include medical devices (for both vital signs and imagery), clinical observations, and laboratory and pathology, such as from serum blood draws resulting in comprehensive metabolic panels and tissue samples for pathology assessments [8].

As was discussed in Chapter 1, there are multiple sources of information that lead to an understanding of the state and diagnosis of a patient condition. All data sources taken together combined with the training of the clinicians and allied healthcare providers, together with protocols and guidelines, establish the approach to treatment and management of the patient. When describing the sources of contemporaneous patient care data, the accuracy and timeliness of these data weigh into the evolution and stability of the patient. Specific examples serve to flesh out how the data obtained from PCDs provide a real-time and continuous mechanism for assessing the state over time.

An example wherein the combination of data from multiple sources results in an integrated assessment of the patient is in the use of early warning scores (EWS) that combine vital signs measurements with observations. Table 2.3 summarizes an example of one early warning score that combines measurements of heart rate, respiration, urine output, and patient conscious awareness.

Early warning scores are typically used to identify patients who are decompensating in cardiovascular and respiratory function, such as through the effects of systemic inflammatory response syndrome (SIRS):

Table 2.3 Example of an Early Warning Score Calculation Table [46]

Individual early warning score	3	2	1	0	1	2	3
Respiration (breaths per minute)		≤8		9–14	15–20	21–29	≥29
Heart rate (per minute)		≤40	41–50	51–100	101–110	111–129	≥129
Systolic BP (mmHg)	≤70	71–80	81–100	101–119			≥200
Urine output (mL/kg/hr)		<0.5					
Temperature (°C)		≤35	35.1–36	36.1–38	38.1–38.5	≥38.6	
Neurological assessment				Alert and Oriented (A)	Reacts to voice (V)	Reacts to pain (P)	Unresponsive (U)
Total score (4 or higher, or individual score 3) = Respiration + Heart rate + Systolic BP + Urine output + Temperature + Neurological assessment.							

Early warning system (EWS) scores are tools used by hospital care teams to recognize the early signs of clinical deterioration in order to initiate early intervention and management, such as increasing nursing attention, informing the provider, or activating a rapid response or medical emergency team. [53, 54]

Thus, patient care device data augment other clinical information, such as clinical observations, to provide a systemwide assessment of patient state.

2.6 Chapter Summary

Patient care device data collection has increasingly become a part of the fabric of EHR and HIT system deployment. Data gathered from PCDs are often used to supplement or supplant manual charting, and provides for more complete, objective, and accurate means of gathering vital signs information from medical devices associated with the patient to recipient HIT systems to augment bedside clinical decision-making. Integrating data from PCDs at the point of care is particularly important for technologically dependent classes of patients, such as those in the operating room or intensive care unit settings, or in cases in which a reliable means of regular data capture would assist the clinical decision-making process, such as in cases where patients are at risk for sudden respiratory or cardiovascular decompensation.

Today, many medical devices still do not universally conform to specific messaging interface standards, such as HL7®, but, rather, rely on proprietary, vendor-specific interface communication. Many medical devices communicate over serial ports and require medical device intermediaries (i.e., MDI platforms) to translate proprietary data from medical devices at the point of care into the more standardized communication and messaging format acceptable for the EHR and HIT systems. Proprietary, medical device manufacturer-specific communication protocols may also imply proprietary or non-standard messaging semantics involving vendor-specific lexicons that need to be translated into a common base lexicon to facilitate common interpretation by the EHR or HIT system. The importance of a common messaging standard and lexicon is vital as these PCD data are used for clinical decision making. Furthermore, data collection from certain classes of PCDs, such as physiological monitors, can be accomplished using monitoring gateways or concentrators that relieve the requirement of point of care serial PCD communication.

Finally, it is necessary to understand patient context: how the patient's past medical history, medication record, and history of the present illness translate into the current physiology and state of the patient. Data combined from multiple sources facilitates a well-rounded understanding of the patient; where the patient has been; what brings he or she to the hospital now; how his or her state has evolved as measured through the vital signs. All information together helps to flesh out the narrative leading to diagnosis, treatment, and guides continuing patient care.

Chapter 3

Alarms and Clinical Surveillance

3.1 Introduction to Alarms

In 2011, a combination of governmental and non-governmental agencies, including the Association for the Advancement of Medical Instrumentation (AAMI), the US Food and Drug Administration (FDA), The Joint Commission (TJC), American College of Clinical Engineering (ACCE), and ECRI held a joint summit focused on the issues surrounding alarm signal annunciation from medical devices [27]. This *Alarm Summit* sought to raise awareness of the challenges associated with medical device alarm signal noise, particularly surrounding the high volume of false or non-clinically actionable alarm signals—referred to as false or nuisance alarms. Alarm signals then and today continue to be a source of distraction for already-burdened bedside clinicians, and pose a significant patient safety risk [27, 49–52].

The Alarm Summit gave voice to many stakeholders (clinical, technical, healthcare systems, and vendors), and shed a spotlight on the issues of alarm fatigue, false positive alarm signals, false negative events, and the challenges faced by clinicians in responding to medical device alarms. The decision as to whether to respond to an alarm or not is one of identifying whether what is seen or heard is real or not. A false alarm is one in which no valid triggering has taken place in the patient or equipment yet is issued based on some condition other than a true clinically underlying cause. This does not mean that the alarm is invalid, only that there may be no emergent clinically actionable cause requiring immediate intervention. Yet, there can be many reasons for alarm signal annunciation from patient care devices.

For example, relative to the cause of an alarm, alarm signal annunciation may [30, 53]:

1. Detect life-threatening causes.
2. Detect imminent or impending danger based upon the trend or trajectory of one or more measured parameter(s)
3. Provide diagnostic information about the state of the patient that may not necessarily be associated with parameters out-of-specification.
4. Detect medical device malfunctions or issues (e.g.: calibration errors, battery alerts, kinked tubing).
5. Be correlated with other contextual patient information to help identify the true cause of an alarm.
6. Be combined with high-frequency data, such as electrocardiogram (ECG) waveforms, to improve understanding of alarm root cause.
7. Indicate that the patient is trending towards an adverse event.

Despite much effort and time spent in researching ways to reduce false or nuisance alarms, seeking a more clinically actionable alarm signal remains a continuing challenge. To wit, the Anesthesia Patient Safety Foundation (APSF) published in its newsletter in 2019:

> Life support devices (e.g., ventilators and cardiopulmonary bypass machines) … employ alarms to alert health care providers to potentially life-threatening failures. These two alarm types (i.e., physiologic and device function) lead to a high frequency of alarms in the clinical setting … in one study of patients undergoing procedures, 8,975 alarms occurred during 25 consecutive procedures … [averaging] of 359 alarms … recorded during each procedure, or approximately 1.2 alarms per minute. [54]

In a citation of one of their recent papers, the *American Journal of Critical Care Nurses* reported that, despite the advancements that have been taken over the years relative to improvements in physiological and other forms of bedside monitoring technology, such advancements "may have improved the accuracy of alarm systems and simplified much of the data collection but haven't affected the clinical relevance of alarms" [55].

The authors performed a meta-study that sought an integrative review of 12 alarms reported from 1986 through 2015, concluding that "… only 5 to 13 percent [of total annotated alarms] were clinically relevant" [64].

Hence, innovative approaches are required to address the problem of alarm and alert fatigue, and the thesis of this author's argument is that bringing improved context to the point of care decision-making process through the use of bedside PCD data that are continuously obtained and assessed, is one such innovative approach. As will be shown in the remainder of this chapter, the challenges associated with false alarms and with differentiating true positive events from false positive events can be akin to finding a "needle in a haystack", unless appropriate context is brought to bear in the clinical decision-making process.

3.2 False and Nuisance Alarms

As was just described, and based on the reference literature, most alarm signals annunciated by bedside patient care devices do not carry clinically actionable content. When an alarm sounds but has no clinically actionable meaning, this is referred to as a false positive alarm or, simply, a false alarm: an alarm signal without an underlying cause necessitating clinical intervention at the time of the annunciation of the event. One metastudy reported in the American Journal of Critical Care, *AJCC*, that "consistently low proportions of patient alarms requiring clinician action (5%–13%)" [56].

Yet, as so many clinical alarm signals (the vast majority), are not clinically actionable, the challenge remains over identifying clinical relevance, as the definitions surrounding this are fuzzy: what may be relevant to one person may be irrelevant to another. Furthermore, can the PCDs themselves provide prompts into the potential root causes of alarm signal annunciation, thereby improving the "intelligence" of the alarm signal? [56, 57]

Methods thus far for improving clinical relevance of alarms have been empirical: such methods that reduce the audible and reported quantities of alarm signals transmitted to nursing and other clinical staff have tended to focus on heuristics, or using simple limit settings that result in alarm signal annunciations when a particular threshold is breached [29]. For example, setting pulse oximetry threshold limits based on the physician (or protocol) prescribed limit settings for any given patient is one such heuristic approach. This approach to mitigating alarm signal annunciations amounts to adjusting the limit setting threshold in order to de-sensitize the alarm, thereby reducing overall alarm signal annunciations. While this approach results in reduced *sensitivity**, the impact on alarm signal *specificity†* becomes questionable. That is, if the impact on an alarm signal annunciation is made more insensitive by adjusting (i.e., widening) alarm signal thresholds in order to squelch the alarm signals that are annunciated, then the likelihood of missing a true event increases as well since there is no insight obtained as to whether widening alarm limits will cause the missing of events. In other words, simply widening the limits merely desensitizes detection, but does not provide innovative knowledge into whether the condition is or is not present. This latter concern—that of missing a true event—refers to false negatives and can have deadly consequences in the patient care setting. To illustrate the importance of responding to truly clinically actionable events, and as an example of the importance of identifying truly actionable clinical alarms, between 2009 and 2012, The Joint Commission received 98 voluntarily reported sentinel events, 80 of which were associated with a medical device alarm cause. That is, either harm or death resulted from these sentinel events and, at the core, a medical or PCD alarm was the root cause [56]. Mechanisms to improve specificity have been employed including tailoring or customizing alarms to specific patients [56, 58].

Two approaches for reducing alarm sensitivity include widening parameter thresholds or employing sustained delays (that is, delaying an alarm signal annunciation until the alarm condition or threshold breach has been experienced for a minimum amount of time). The sustained delay, it is postulated, operates from the perspective that if an alarm condition occurs and does not selfcorrect for a predefined period of time, then that alarm condition must be real. This, of course, is an assumption. Some sustained delays can exceed 60 seconds [59]. This can certainly reduce the overall quantity of alarm signal annunciations. On the other hand, if alarm signal annunciations are made to be too insensitive, the chance of introducing a more dangerous condition—that of the *false negative event*—can result. A false negative event occurs when one fails to recognize an event that truly is happening and carries with it clinical significance or relevance necessitating some form of intervention.

In 2015, AAMI chronicled experiences and solution approaches to begin to address the challenges of alarm signals, with a key pilot being the Dartmouth-Hitchcock Medical Center. One key finding was that the

---

* Sensitivity: a measure of how often a correct result is observed when the effect actually exists.
† Specificity: a measure of how often a negative result is observed when the effect does not actually exist.

introduction of 30-second sustained notification delays in alarm signals would reduce their alarm burden [29, p. 23]. Still, the use of sustained notification delays (recall: wait a pre-defined period of time before responding to the alarm signal) or methods will not universally resolve the challenge of false negative events.

Some recommendations for alleviating alarm burden vary based on local protocols and on empirical findings that vary by health system, by department, and even by clinicians. For instance, some recommendations focus on 10-second or 20-second alarm signal sustained notification delays and tailoring alarms based on the type of care unit or even by patient. For example, a multi-year initiative by Texas Children's Hospital resulted in a 66% reduction in code red alarm signals and staff emergencies [29, p. 32].

Measurement artifact, or noise, has also been cited as a source of false alarms, particularly with electrocardiogram electrodes. Empirical causes for a measurement artifact have been reported, and those associated with electrocardiogram electrodes and pulse oximetry have been identified as a key cause [60].

Alarm signals associated with an electrocardiogram measurement artifact include:

1. Poor electrode preparation and placement.
2. Inadequate or absent electrode change-out scheduling.
3. Broken equipment, such as electrode lead wires.

Alarm signals associated with a pulse oximetry measurement artifact include:

1. Pulse oximetry sensor cuff placement.
2. Cables disconnected or broken.
3. Patient conditions such as cold fingers, nail polish, or poor perfusion.

Thus, clinically actionable alarm signals can be the result of technical malfunctions as well as events based on the values of alarm signals (e.g.: low or high heart rate; low or high respiration rate; low oxygen saturation). Hence, building one-size-fits-all alarm signals is an oversimplification to a complex problem. Yet, customization of alarm signal thresholds is also burdensome and does not carry sufficient information to be able to identify clinically actionable alarm signals. So, something more informative is required – more on the order of a flexible manner or framework in which to define alarms that can be applied to as few as a single patient or as many as are deemed clinically appropriate.

3.3 Paving the Way for More Intelligent Alarms

The basic objective of an alarm signal is to provide a notification of an event in the clinical setting when that event occurs. Alarm signals are a means of identifying when measured values from PCDs deviate from expected or *a priori* identified normal ranges. For example, PCDs issue alarms that are normally set to a standard default based on the practice of medicine and/ or defined by published guidelines and protocols and are further refined or customized based upon best practices, learnings, policies, studies, and the prescriptions of attending physicians.

The effect of alarm signals on clinical care has been studied over the past decade, and the results are notable, as this example from Johns Hopkins Medical Center illustrates:

> Hospital staff are exposed to an average of 350 alarms per bed per day, based on a sample from an intensive care unit at the Johns Hopkins Hospital in Baltimore. [51]

The problem with attenuating alarm signals is achieving the balance between communicating the essential, patient safety-specific information that will provide proper notification to clinical staff of an actionable event while minimizing the excess, spurious, and non-emergent events that are not indicative of a threat to patient safety. In the absence of contextual information, the conservative approach is usually to err on the side of treating an alarm signal as actionable because the risk of missing an emergent alarm signal or notification carries with it the potential for high cost (e.g.: patient harm or death).

For example, suppose that heart rate (HR) is being measured continuously, as shown in Figure 3.1. This plot shows heart rate relatively constant at 70 beats per minute (bpm) with two "spikes": one at 400 seconds, with a value of 150 bpm and another at 600 seconds, with a value of approximately 40 bpm. Two signal threshold values are overlaid on the diagram: one for tachycardia (high sinus heart rate), $HR_{tachy}^{thr} = 100$ bpm; the second for brady-cardia (low sinus heart rate), $HR_{brady}^{thr} = 60$ bpm.

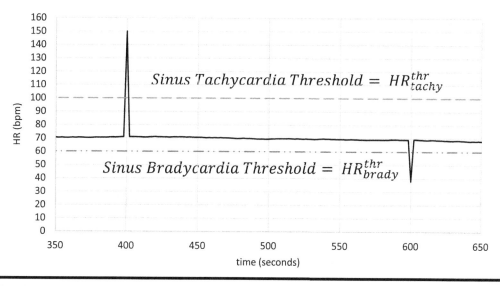

Figure 3.1 Measured heart rate (HR) showing examples of limit violations—limit threshold breaches.

When a measurement exceeds the thresholds, as shown in the diagram, the result would be an alarm associated with that event. Here, one sinus tachycardia and one bradycardia alarm would be annunciated at 400- and 600-seconds, respectively. The annunciation of these alarms is based on the mathematical comparison between the HR measurement and the HR threshold. The threshold stands as a crude proxy for a clinically actionable event: it is surmised that if the measurement breaches the threshold, the event represents something clinically relevant to which a response is necessary—for example, a patient who is truly experiencing atrial fibrillation or ventricular tachycardia. The alarm threshold alone makes no clinical distinction as to whether the threshold breach is due to some truly emergent event, or, say, because the patient moved in the bed.

In practice, whether the alarm reflects an event that carries a truly clinically actionable meaning or not depends on many factors including by what means the measurement was obtained, what conditions associated with the patient were active at the time of the measurement (e.g., patient movement), accuracy of the measurement (i.e., presence of, or lack of artifact), sensor and electrode integrity, and other factors. Because, as has been documented, there is a significant likelihood that alarm signals generated based on simple threshold breaches will carry no relevant clinical value, mechanisms and methods need to be employed to increase the sensitivity and specificity of such alarm signals. Ergo, studies by various clinical researchers have revealed that many alarms annunciated in the high acuity environments (e.g., intensive care) carry little clinical meaning, and, thus, lack informative skill at identifying valuable clinical information [29, 31].

When an alarm signal is annunciated the direct and simple assumption is that the alarm signal is a call to action associated with an event that requires a response. In other words, the alarm signal is assumed to be genuine. Thus, the assumption is that in truth, if an alarm signal annunciates, then an event requiring action must have occurred. Otherwise, if no alarm signal annunciates, then no event occurred that requires action.

When an alarm signal annunciation is observed, the decision as to whether the observed annunciation is true or false is at hand and the default reaction is that an intervention is necessary. In actuality, the observer may be mistaken, or, in the case of an alarm signal annunciation, the event may occur without carrying clinical import. In other words, the alarm signal may be wrong. For instance, if a patient adjusts himself or herself in a hospital bed, this can result in the movement of sensors or electrodes placed on the fingers or body that measure heart rate or peripheral oxygen saturation levels. If these sensors are disturbed, they can cause a change in the measurement of parameters which create significant signal artifact in a signal measurement threshold breach and a concomitant annunciation of an alarm signal. Here, the alarm signal cause is movement of a sensor that resulted in a change in a reading or measurement that was sufficiently large to trigger the alarm based on the measured value from the sensor. But, while the alarm signal is annunciated, there is no clinically actionable event requiring intervention: once the patient settles back down, the signal may return to normal. This alarm annunciation example represents a false alarm.

On the other hand, if the alarm signal change was due to an actual increase in heart rate measurement (say, a run of sinus tachycardia, atrial fibrillation, or supraventricular tachycardia), then the alarm signal would be genuine, or clinically actionable. In any case, the unknowing clinician would be notified. The implication is an increased burden on clinicians which can result in burnout, and even missing truly actionable events as clinicians become insensitive to the many non-clinically actionable alarm signals annunciated within the environment.

In the 2019 edition of its Top 10 Health Technology Hazards, the ECRI cited "alarms, alerts and notification overload" as necessitating further investigation [13].

The problem of alarm overload is well known. Just as important to consider, however, is the global notification burden—that is, the combination of alarms, alerts, and notifications from all sources, not just from a single medical device.

ECRI acknowledged the challenges of physician burnout and detecting changes in patient condition in their *Top 10 Patient Safety Concerns* [12].

Furthermore, AAMI, in its Clinical Alarm Management Compendium, summarized the "top five gaps in alarm-management related knowledge," to include (1) "lack of documentation and data to analyze reported events and near misses to understand root problem(s)" and (2) "lack of evidence-based rationale for the configurations of alarm settings" [29, p. 11].

Armed with the evidence from the field, research and the history of safety concerns surrounding false alarms and the impact they have had on both clinicians and patients and the healthcare setting, it is now time to take a closer look at identifying true and false alarm signal events in the context of clinical alarms.

3.4 Defining Actionable and Non-Actionable Alarms

The alarm management concern surrounds the issuing of alarm signals from PCDs in proximity to the patient at the point of care. Patient care device alarms issued in high acuity environments include those from physiological monitors, telemetry monitors, infusion pumps, mechanical ventilators, and other specialty devices (e.g.: intra-aortic balloon pumps, hemodialysis machines, etc.) The concerns surrounding PCD alarms and their effects on clinicians and patients was summarized in the preceding section and through the references cited [29, 51, 61, 62]. From the patient safety perspective, one CBS news report, quoting the US FDA, cited "more than 500 deaths potentially linked with hospital alarms between January 2005 and June 2010. ... [including reports of] malfunctions and in some cases the connection to a death is only tenuous" [63].

Despite these concerns and real adverse events, identifying and solving the false alarm problem to mitigate noise or alarm fatigue requires cross-interaction between mathematical analysis and clinical insight. Those knowledgeable or otherwise familiar with statistics and the concept of Type I (i.e., false positive events) and Type II (false negative events) error conditions will understand that identifying true positive events (actionable alarms) from false positive events (non-actionable alarms) has a potential consequence in terms of a cost in sensitivity and specificity. In the healthcare setting, missing true alarms (i.e., false negatives, or Type II errors) can translate into catastrophic results (patient harms or death). In order to better understand these concepts, a treatment of false alarms follows. Once this understanding is established mathematically, a translation into clinical context can occur.

As an example of the occurrence of a false alarm in the clinical setting, consider the scenario in which a monitored patient moves in bed and dislodges a pulse oximetry sensor from his or her finger. This results in a disruption of the signal from that sensor. In such a case, action is required to correct the sensor position. The sensor ceases to report additional measurements, and this results in an alarm signal annunciation indicating sensor off finger. This action merits an intervention to reapply the pulse oximetry sensor. But, the reason for the intervention is not because of a clinically actionable measurement (i.e., a desaturation event), but, rather, to correct the position of the sensor on the finger. Nevertheless, action on the part of the clinician is still required to correct the event. Thus, the alarm signal can:

- Refer to a clinically actionable event (i.e., a desaturation);
- Refer to a necessary intervention to correct an aberration (i.e., pulse oximetry sensor off finger); or,
- Refer to a non-actionable event associated with artifact (i.e., movement of the sensor on the finger which results in a temporary loss of signal that is regained once the patient movement stops).

In the context here, clinical intervention is intended to mean an action that is necessary to save a life or otherwise prevent harm to the patient, which can involve either responding to a true desaturation event, or correcting the loss-of-signal problem that can also mask a true event in which signal loss results in missing a true event. Thus, in both the cases of a desaturation event and sensor dislodgement, clinical intervention is necessary, albeit for different reasons: either the event represented a true desaturation, or the dislodgement could result in missing a true clinical event because no measurements would be obtained, thus resulting in gaps in surveillance.

One can refer to the conditions indicative of a true event (true alarm) or a false event (false alarm) with the aid of a mnemonic diagram which lays out the conditions associated with what is referred to in statistics as the *null hypothesis*. The null hypothesis is a test of statistical significance and asserts that no significant difference exists between certain specified populations and a specific test case, and that any differences that do exist are due to errors in sampling or experimentation. Hence, as relates to the challenge of determining whether an annunciated alarm signal reflects a truly clinically actionable event or not, the annunciation of the alarm signal occurring either carries clinical significance or it does not. The identification of alarms as being real or not follows from hypothesis testing. Consider that the null hypothesis, H_o, establishes that the status quo is true: the observed data are expected based upon the population or sample of data already available. Given this hypothesis, then, the decisions to be evaluated include the following:

- If the null hypothesis is <u>true</u>, and we <u>do not reject it</u>, then this is a <u>correct</u> decision.
- If the null hypothesis is <u>false</u>, and we <u>reject it</u>, then this is a <u>correct</u> decision.
- If the null hypothesis is <u>true</u>, and we <u>reject it</u>, then this is a <u>Type I</u> error.
- If the null hypothesis is <u>false</u>, and we <u>fail to reject it</u>, then this is a <u>Type II</u> error.

These decisions can be represented in a decision table, Table 3.1. In alarm signal annunciation, one can consider by analogy the null hypothesis that there is no clinically actionable event occurring with a patient. Then, the alternative hypothesis is that there is a clinically actionable event occurring with a patient. This is represented as follows:

$$H_o: \text{no clinically actionable event occurring}$$

$$H_a: \text{clinically actionable event occurring}$$

The Type I error occurs when the "evidence" leads one to reject a true null hypothesis and accept a false alternative hypothesis. An example related to

Table 3.1 Type I and II Decision Table Based on Null and Alternate Hypothesis Testing [64]

Null hypothesis/alternative hypothesis table	Reject H_o (i.e., accept H_a)	Fail to reject H_o
H_o is true	Type I error	Correct decision
H_o is false (i.e., H_a is true)	Correct decision	Type II error

alarm signal annunciations is as follows: the null hypothesis states that there is no clinically actionable event requiring intervention. But, the (false) alternative hypothesis is accepted. Hence, the alternative hypothesis is selected incorrectly: an alarm signal annunciation occurs despite the fact that there is no clinically actionable event occurring.

The Type II error occurs when the "evidence" leads one to fail to reject a null hypothesis that is false. In other words, one may think that the status quo is that there is no clinically actionable event requiring intervention, when, in fact, there is. This is (incorrectly) failing to reject the null hypothesis when the alternative hypothesis is indeed true.

Thus, in brief:

■ With a Type I error, we reject a null hypothesis that is true.
■ With a Type II error, we fail to reject a null hypothesis that is false.

Thus, in representing the various possible outcomes, one considers the observation of the alarm signal (that is, whether one hears and responds to it or not), the alarm signal is annunciated or not, and when annunciated, it either carries true clinical import or not. The possible conditions relate to the four inner boxes in the diagram of Table 3.2:

■ True positive (TP): an alarm signal occurs, and that alarm signal refers to an event that is truly clinically actionable.
■ False positive (FP): an alarm signal occurs, but that alarm signal refers to an event that is not truly clinically actionable.

Table 3.2 Null Hypothesis Table Identifying an Alarm Signal as Truly Clinically Actionable

False alarm null hypothesis table	*Alarm signal not clinically actionable*	*Alarm signal clinically actionable*	
Alarm signal occurs	False positive (FP) Type I error	True positive (TP)	Total test positive (TTP)
Alarm signal does not occur	True negative (TN)	False negative (FN) Type II error	Total test negative (TTN)
	Total non-clinically actionable alarm signals (TNCA)	Total clinically actionable alarm signals (TCA)	Total clinically and non-clinically actionable alarms

- False negative (FN): an alarm signal does not occur, but there is a truly clinically actionable event occurring that requires intervention.
- True negative (TN): an alarm signal does not occur, and there is no clinically actionable event occurring requiring intervention.

The best-case situation would refer to those cases in which alarms ONLY refer to true positive events, and the lack of alarms ONLY refer to when no clinical intervention is required. As was discussed previously, many events occur that do not require clinical intervention but do cause an alarm signal to annunciate. Hence, a preponderance of false positive events is typically the case. As a key objective in alarm signal remediation is to reduce the number of false alarms or nuisance alarms, this can be accomplished by decreasing sensitivity. Yet, decreasing sensitivity without further innovation in terms of knowledge or context has the effect of increasing the likelihood of missing actual events, resulting in an increased quantity of false negative events (i.e., the events are actually missed occurrences but there is no corresponding alarm signal to notify the clinical user). Thus, the danger here is that false negative events can be deleterious to the patient. Whereas increasing sensitivity can result in the potential for alarm fatigue as the clinician is now responding to more non-clinically actionable events (i.e., nuisance alarms), descreasing sensitivity may obscure events that are truly clinically actionable, and the patient may experience a truly adverse event that requires intervention but for which intervention does not occur as the event goes undetected. Thus, in the former case, the clinician is saved the aggravation of responding to non-clinically-actionable events. But, in the latter case, patient safety may be jeopardized. A balancing between the false positives and false negatives is clearly necessary. Or, better yet, maintaining patient safety by minimizing false negatives while improving the alarm accuracy (i.e., reducing false positives). Discussions of reducing false positive events while minimizing the likelihood of false negative events concentrates on the mathematical concepts of *sensitivity* and *specificity*, defined in Equations 3.1 and 3.2 respectively:

$$\text{Sensitivity} = 100\% \times \frac{\text{TP}}{\text{TP} + \text{FN}} \qquad (3.1)$$

$$\text{Specificity} = 100\% \times \frac{\text{TN}}{\text{TN} + \text{FP}} \qquad (3.2)$$

As previously defined, the sensitivity is the probability or fraction indicating that a condition is present among those in which the condition is present. The specificity is the probability or fraction indicating a negative result in those not having the condition.

Two other concepts are now introduced: positive predictive value (PPV) and negative predictive value (NPV), given by Equations 3.3 and 3.4, respectively:

$$PPV = 100\% \times \frac{TP}{TP + FP} \tag{3.3}$$

$$NPV = 100\% \times \frac{TN}{TN + FN} \tag{3.4}$$

The positive predictive value represents the probability that alarms, when they annunciate, occur due to truly clinically actionable events. Negative predictive value represents the probability that when no alarm annunciates, there is truly no clinically actionable event occurring.

A simple example can suffice to illustrate the use of Equations (3.1)–(3.4), with the aid of Table 3.3. As shown in this table, the sensitivity and specificity are computed to be 97.1% and 69.2%, respectively, with a PPV and NPV of 28.6% and 96.8%. Here, the numeric values for true positives, false positives, true negatives, and false negatives are selected to show a high sensitivity and high negative predictive value, due principally to the small number of FNs. Yet, the specificity is moderate (69.2%) due to the high number of

Table 3.3 Worked Example of a Null Hypothesis Table

	Alarm signal clinically actionable	Alarm signal not clinically actionable			Sensitivity:	97.09%
Alarm signal occurs	400	400	TTP:	1400	Specificity:	69.23%
Alarm signal does not occur	900	900	TTN:	930	PPV:	28.57%
	TCA	TNCA	Total	2330	NPV:	96.77%
	1330	1030	2330			

TTP, total test positive; TTN, total test negative; PPV, positive predictive value; TCA, total clinically actionable alarm signals; TNCA, total non-clinically actionable alarm signals; NPV, negative predictive value.

false alarms (400). In practice, measurements of alarms and assessments of whether those alarms are truly actionable would need to be made from in situ measurements at the bedside to determine whether an alarm was truly occurring based on PCD measurements.

In the data of Table 3.3, the quantity of non-clinically actionable alarm signals is 400, whereas the quantity of events for which no alarm was annunciated but for which a true intervention was required is 30. The objective is to reduce the false positive rate, while at the same time not causing an increase (or, better yet, to cause a decrease) in the false negative rate. There is a cross-coupling component that is worthy of mention here: if a clinician is distracted by too many false alarms, this can result in missing true events, thereby resulting in an increase in the false negative rate. Hence, a reduction of false positive events is not only about reducing noise irritants in the environment, but it is also about improving the likelihood that any alarm signal that is annunciated does indeed carry with it clinical relevance to the patient.

3.5 Methods for Alarm Signal Creation

Alarm signals generated by standalone PCDs typically annunciate independently of one another. That is, a PCD generates alarm signals based on measurements it receives directly from the sensors attached to the patient without further context or information from other PCDs, observations, or other findings. This is true of standalone PCDs. In those cases in which PCDs are monitored centrally such that the data from multiple PCDs are brought forward from the patient bedside to a central monitoring station, then more context can be derived from the fact that multiple measurements can be co-displayed and employed by the clinician as part of the assessment, decision-making, and monitoring processes. For instance, when a patient's vital signs are monitored using a physiological monitoring device that determines heart rate, blood pressure, peripheral oxygen saturation, and respiration (e.g., respiration from end-tidal capnography), or there may also be situations in which the patient is intubated and receiving therapeutic support from a mechanical ventilator. In the case, for example, of the mechanical ventilator, the measurements and settings obtained from the mechanical ventilator, which may include respirations, tidal volume, flow rate, peak and mean airway pressure, positive end expiratory pressure, and compliance, may also be co-displayed with the physiological monitoring data. These two separate PCDs may provide some overlapping parameter measurements (e.g.: respirations), but generally provide a separate and completely complementary set of findings that, when taken together, paint an overall picture of the patient cardiovascular and respiratory system state over time. As each type of PCD (in this example, physiological monitor and mechanical ventilator) is "knowledgeable" only of the findings it measures, each is effectively blind to the parameters of the other device. As a result, it is the task of the clinician to "integrate" the two (or more) streams of data into the clinical picture comprising the overall state of the patient. Furthermore, alarm signal annunciations created from the separate PCDs are defined with respect to the measured parameters of each separate PCD. This means that insights that may be available from one PCD that would be used to "inform" or provide context around the findings of the second PCD are not generally available (although exceptions exist, such as in the case of interoperable PCDs).

When alarm signals are created based on thresholds associated with the measured parameters obtained from each separate PCD, then the potential exists that multiple alarm signals will annunciate on each PCD independently of one another, with the vast majority of these alarm signals not "benefitting" from the context of other PCDs concomitantly obtaining measurements from the same patient, or from the clinical significance of these measurements. Thus, in monitoring a care unit of patients, each PCD will respond to each patient using the thresholds established on measured parameters prescribed for each patient. If a unit of, say, 20 patients is outfitted with a physiological monitor and a mechanical ventilator per patient, the alarm signals are likely to annunciate from both medical devices associated with a given patient independently of one another. Carrying this idea further, additional PCDs would likewise annunciate alarms independently, adding to the alarm signal annunciation burden in the environment.

Suppose that an approach taken by the clinical staff in a particular critical care unit of a hospital is to deploy customized settings on PCDs so as to tailor or customize alarm signal thresholds in accordance with the needs and behavior of a specific patient. Given a desire to employ tailored or customized thresholds in a standard intensive care unit with, say, 20 patient rooms, each patient room equipped, minimally, with a physiological monitor, the thresholds on each individual monitor would need to be set and managed by clinical staff. Logistically, this would entail visiting each monitor to manually adjust the threshold settings, possibly individually on each patient, depending on the prescribed monitoring of the patient. Making such changes can introduce errors in configuration. Furthermore, the need to return the monitor to the original default settings must be remembered when patients are discharged and new patients are admitted or else settings from a prior patient will exist on the monitors and these settings may not be appropriate for new patients. This can result in the introduction of a hazard: if the incorrect settings are used inadvertently on a patient other than the one for whom they were intended, this can result not only in false alarms, but the possibility of false negatives which, as was discussed previously, can have deadly consequences.

Perhaps another approach should be considered: one that does not introduce logistical hazards into the environment of the busy clinician. Returning again to the concept of continuous monitoring, consider, for example, the identification of hypoventilation, CO_2 narcosis, and sleep apnea, which can occur in certain sedated patients or patients who are receiving pain medication (e.g., opioid medication for postoperative pain management). Let's suppose continuous monitoring of respirations and end-tidal carbon dioxide through capnography is taking place, together with pulse, pulse oximetry, and blood pressure measurements occurring concomitantly. Each measurement represents a single value (scalar) with a given or known threshold that defines the guard rails or limits of acceptability for each parameter. As measurements are obtained, changes and variations in measured parameter values occur rather continuously over time. These variations may or may not be clinically significant. Yet, variations in single parameter measured values may not be a good indicator of adverse events, such as patient respiratory compromise in the case of a sedated patient. Hence, monitoring of multiple parameters to assess their interrelationships is an important consideration, as multiple independent measurements can be correlated and associated with clinically significant criteria that, when evaluated together, can yield important early indicators of pending decompensation [15, 21, 22, 65–67]. For instance, observing how heart rate variations occur with changes in pulse oximetry; or, respiration changes with respect to changes in end-tidal carbon dioxide and pulse oximetry. When multiple parameters change in a manner consistent with their physiological interrelationships, the likelihood that all changes are due to artifact is less than single parameter variations alone.

The following subsections focus on methods of alarm signal annunciation associated with single parameter measurement in comparison with multiple parameters taken simultaneously to identify and improve the specificity of alarm signals.

3.6 Alarm Signals Based on Limit Threshold Breaches

Limit threshold breaches are, perhaps, the most direct and simplest form of alarm signal annunciation trigger. Limit threshold breaches annunciate when a measurement from a specific parameter exceeds a known threshold on that parameter. For example, when a heart rate measurement exceeds a tachycardia threshold of, say, 130 beats per minute, or when a respiration measurement falls below a lower limit of 6 breaths per minute. Many PCDs can provide default settings of limit thresholds on parameters.

One challenge that may be experienced is when limit thresholds need to be managed individually or adjusted on a per patient basis. It is much more difficult for clinical staff to modify thresholds on each patient and then to remember to return these values to defaults based on hospital policies or clinical guidelines. As discussed previously, the workflow impacts associated with accomplishing this can be overwhelming to a busy staff. Limit threshold breaches have their place in identifying deviations of measured patient values against set guard rails based on clinical practice. Yet, alarm signals based on limit threshold breaches do not necessarily provide insight into the context of a patient's condition in that measured parameters tend to vary in relationship with one another and it is these interrelationships, or behaviors among parameter values, that can provide earlier indicators of patient deterioration [16, 33, 68, 69].

A standard complaint surrounding alarm signals based on limit threshold breaches is that they can result in a large number of false alarm signals being issued on a patient, principally because measurements can exceed alarm limit thresholds for many reasons that are not related to true or clinically actionable events. That is, the alarm signal exceeds or breaches the established limit threshold but then self-corrects, and the reason for the breach may be transient and not repeated. If the system sensitivity is set so that an alarm will be issued instantaneously when an event occurs, then a large quantity of limit threshold breach alarms will likely be issued, most of which are non-actionable. An example illustrating a situation in which alarm signal limit threshold values are breached is shown in Figure 3.2. Causes of these threshold breaches can include artifact induced by the movement of the patient, movement of the sensors (e.g., nasal cannula, pulse oximetry probes, etc.), and aberrations associated with the equipment (e.g., calibration errors or disconnects). A key point in the case of single limit threshold breaches is that the deviations above the set limit values self-correct by the next measurement. In Figure 3.2, a deviation or threshold breach occurs at

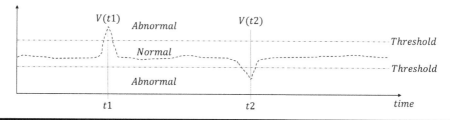

Figure 3.2 Simple display of limit threshold breach alarms when the value of a measurement exceeds a specified threshold, moving from an area of normal range to that of abnormal range. This is the case when a measurement exceeds the limit threshold associated with the normal and abnormal range.

time $t1$ and then another breach occurs at time $t2$. The values of the measured signal are $V(t1)$ and $V(t2)$, respectively. The two events may be uncorrelated or correlated. Yet, the fact that the earlier alarm signal (i.e., at time $t1$ occurs) is immaterial to the annunciation of the signal at the time $t2$.

3.7 Alarm Signals Based on Non-Self-Correcting Measurements

The concept of a persistent alarm signal—one that does not self-correct within a particular amount of time—is defined wherein a threshold breach must be continuously maintained for a period of time (some number of seconds) before an alarm is issued. The upper and lower plots of Figure 3.3

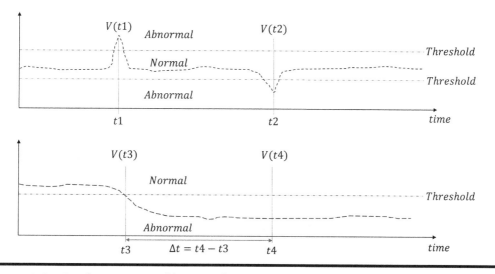

Figure 3.3 Persistent, non-self-correcting alarm signal versus a limit threshold breach signal.

compare the difference between limit threshold breaches and non-self-correcting threshold breaches. The logic behind an alarm signal based on non-self-correcting measurements is that the condition that is causing the parameter to breach the threshold is not aberrant but there is some specific cause that is persistent. The alarm signal resulting from non-self-correcting measurements can result in fewer overall false alarms. Yet, there is also no guarantee that the presence of alarm signals based on this methodology will mean there is a clinically actionable event. The likelihood is greater that there is a cause for events that is not spurious, but these events may not be clinically actionable.

An example of a cause that is not immediately detrimental to the patient would be the dislodgement of a pulse oximetry finger sensor resulting in a poor measurement. Another example would be kinked or dislodged nasal cannula tubing, or a failing measurement sensor. The cause is certainly actionable in these two cases, but it is not necessarily indicative of immediate danger to the patient. On the other hand, the cause may have genuine clinical import. For instance, an apnea (no breath) alarm may be issued after judging a sustained low or zero respiration rate measurement for 30 seconds.

In Figure 3.3, the alarm based on non-self-correcting measurements is triggered when the duration of the signal measurement below a defined threshold exceeds a time duration given by Δt. The signal breaches a threshold at time t3 and remains below the signal threshold through at least time t4. The annunciation of the alarm occurs when the signal remains below the threshold continuously for at least the time interval given by t4-t3, and this interval exceeds the time duration threshold. Both the time duration and the signal thresholds are variables that can be defined to initiate the alarm signal annunciation. Thus, if the measured signal deviates from thresholds for a time period greater than or equal to the identified duration, Δt, then the alarm would be annunciated if, as per Equation 3.5:

$$V(t_i) \leq V^{\text{thr}} \ \forall t_i \tag{3.5}$$

This expression states that if each consecutive measurement within a sample is less than or equal to the threshold, then the alarm signal would be annunciated. An example of this technique is also illustrated in Figure 3.4.

In the example illustrated here, the oxygen saturation measurement deviates below a specific threshold for a time period Δt. Thus, an alarm signal annunciation will result if the condition of Equation 3.6 is met:

$$SpO_2(t_i) \leq SpO_2^{\text{thr}} \ \forall t_i \tag{3.6}$$

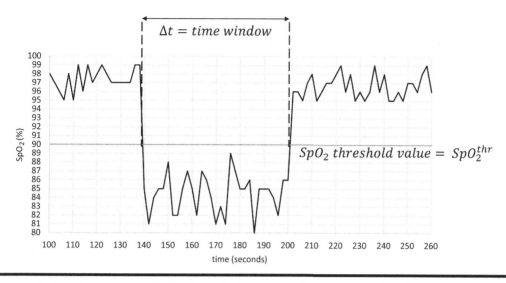

Figure 3.4 Alarm annunciation based on a non-self-correcting signal over a specific time period. (Data source: author.)

Equation 3.6 states that the alarm signal will annunciate only when all measurements in a set meet the criteria. That is, when all measurements consecutively are below the signal threshold. This is what is meant by the term "self-correct": if a measurement returns to normal after a short period of time (i.e., the next measurement or within several measurements below some time window of interest, such as 30 seconds), then the alarm signal will not annunciate: the assumption is that the condition causing the aberrant measurement no longer exists. Yet, if the measurements persist in terms of violating the signal threshold and the time limit associated with this aberration exceeds some critical window, then the alarm signal will annunciate.

3.8 Alarm Signals Based on Deviations from the Historical Trend

As has been shown, threshold based alarm signals are a straightforward method for identifying an actionable event based on deviations outside of known thresholds or guardrails. The threshold based alarm signal type is not very specific and may result in excessive alarm signal annunciations. A variant on the threshold-based alarm signal and the persistent (or non-self-correcting) alarm signal that is a logical extension of both is an alarm signal based on a historical trend. A signal that deviates from its historical trend may be cause for intervention as a change in the historical state (recall the concept of the state vector from Chapter 1) indicates a variation that may not be expected. Several approaches can be taken to evaluate a deviation of a signal with respect to a historical trend:

1) Look for a deviation of any signal measurement with respect to previous history or historical trend.
2) Look for a change in the slope of the signal with respect to previous history or the historical trend.
3) Look for a change in the baseline of the signal with respect to previous history or the historical trend.

The historical trend alarm signal and the non-self-correcting alarm signal share some common behaviors in the fact that measurements are considered over time. In the historical trend alarm signal, the trajectory of the measured parameter follows some correlated (i.e., not random) pathway over time. This represents the history of the signal. Figure 3.5 illustrates the case of a measurement deviating from the historical baseline. Here, that running baseline is a signal average over a specific interval (say, 1 minute in the past). The value that constitutes a significant deviation can be defined as a fixed deviation, such as a fractional deviation with respect to the mean or some other measure, and is somewhat arbitrary but can be also be computed from the statistics of the prior signal measurements. For example, a calculation

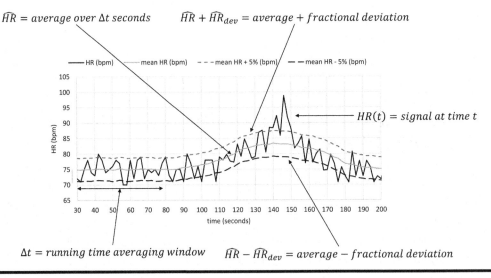

Figure 3.5 A signal (heart rate) that follows a historical trend. When a significant deviation occurs in the measured signal, such as a deviation from the mean of the signal, then this can be a trigger for an alarm signal annunciation.

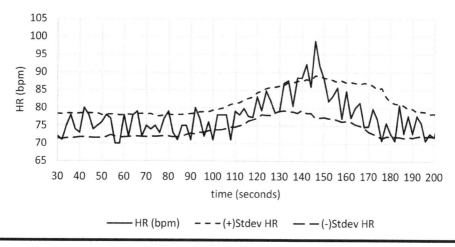

Figure 3.6   Running average (HR) with +/– standard deviation. (Data source: author.)

of the historical sample standard deviation can identify whether a new measurement deviates with respect to the historical signal by a significant amount, as shown in Figure 3.6.

Alternatively, a change in baseline measurements may be cause for notification, such as is illustrated in Figure 3.7, in which a pulse oximetry measurement changes from one mean or average value to another in a relatively short time frame (i.e., several minutes). Such a change may have a non-clinical cause, but it also may be due to some clinical reason. So, depending on the importance of such a change as determined by the clinician, this event may merit an intervention.

A change in trend, such as the increased heart rate of the patient under consideration in Figure 3.8, is also a potential reason for intervention. If a

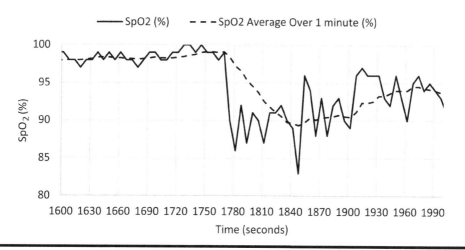

Figure 3.7   An SpO$_2$ signal "finding" a new baseline. (Data source: author.)

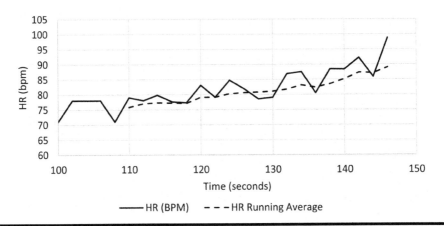

Figure 3.8   An HR alarm signal evolving over a historical trend. (Data source: author.)

measurement is following a normal trend when an observed significant* increase or decrease from that baseline takes place over a given time window without clinically attributable cause (e.g.: medication administration with expected effect), then this, too, would be a reason for an intervention.

Again, note that a difference between the alarm signal based on non-self-correcting measurements and the various types of historical trend alarm signals are all concerned with the time interval of consideration as the annunciation of the alarm occurs after a period in which all signal measurements consecutively deviate from (i.e., above or below) the threshold value or a baseline limit setting. In the historical trend alarm signal, the time period, Δt, indicates the past history in which the comparison is made relative to the current behavior of the particular parameter under consideration. Furthermore, the quantity or amount by which a signal deviates from the historical running average may also be considered, either as a fraction relative to the baseline, in relation to a statistical measurement, such as the sample standard deviation computed over the averaging interval, or as a slope in relation to the baseline measurement.

Define the average signal value over an interval given between t_i and $t_i + \Delta t_i$ per Equation 3.7 as:

$$\widehat{V}(t) = \frac{1}{N} \sum_{t=t_i-\Delta t}^{t=t_i} V(t) \tag{3.7}$$

---

* Significance is defined prescriptively by the clinician, and may vary from patient to patient. For example, a 5 point drop in oxygen saturation or a 10 point drop or increase in heart rate.

The average value of the signal in Equation 3.7 is then given by $\hat{V}(t)$, which represents the average value at the current time, t. Here, N is a variable representing the number (or quantity) of measurements within the measurement interval under consideration. The quantity of measurements depends on the size of the interval and the frequency with which measurements are obtained during that interval (e.g.: 10 measurements per minute). The average signal is a historical determination of the past Δt measurements.

The alarm signal annunciation will occur when the instantaneous signal deviates from the historical running average by an amount that exceeds the specified deviation. The deviation in the alarm signal that defines the threshold limit is given by Equation 3.8 :

$$V_{\text{dev}} = f \times \hat{V}(t_i + \Delta t) \tag{3.8}$$

The signal deviation, V_{dev}, in Equation 3.8 is a threshold where the multiplication factor, f, can be a fixed value or, alternatively, a fractional deviation with respect to some statistical measurement such as the sample standard deviation of the signal over the historical interval.

Thus, the multiplication factor is defined with respect to Equation 3.9:

$$f = \begin{cases} c_1 \\ c_2 = (c_1 \times \langle statistic \rangle) \end{cases} \tag{3.9}$$

The constant c_1 can be a fixed value representative scale factor associated with the average signal (i.e., the constant could range from 0 to greater than 1). The constant c_2 can represent a scale factor on the running sample statistic employed, such as the sample standard deviation, or median, of the historical signal. Just as the average was computed using Equation 3.7, the sample standard deviation can be computed with the aid of Equation 3.10:

$$\text{StDev}(t_i) = \frac{1}{N-1} \sum_{t=t_i-\Delta t}^{t=t_i} \left(V(t_i) - \hat{V}(t_i - \Delta t)\right)^2 \tag{3.10}$$

Thus, when the instantaneous signal deviates from the historical average, an alarm signal annunciation occurs, corresponding to the mathematical conditions specified by either Equations 3.11 or 3.12, respectively:

$$V(t) \geq \hat{V}(t) + V_{\text{dev}} \tag{3.11}$$

or

$$V(t) \leq \hat{V}(t) - V_{\text{dev}} \qquad (3.12)$$

Recall the heart rate signal of Figure 3.5. The signal of Figure 3.5 uses a signal threshold based on statistics determined from the historical trend of the time-varying parameter measurement. Given the resting heart rate average of 75 beats per minute, a significant increase in this value, such as a measurement of approximately 100 beats per minute, may be of importance to report. Deviations from the historical trend can be indicative of actionable events associated with clinical judgment, and a clinician may opt to be notified of these changes or trajectories over time.

Determining the level of deviation that is clinically significant is, of course, based on the practice of medicine, protocols, training, clinical experience and judgment. The next section will focus on applying these concepts to two or more measured findings simultaneously.

3.9 Multi-Parameter Threshold Alarms: Alarm Signals Based on Two or More Findings

When considering that single-parameter threshold based alarm signal can annunciate because of non-clinically actionable events, an approach that can aid in reducing the effects of single-parameter alarm signal sensitivity and increased specificity is that of considering more parameters simultaneously as part of the alarm signal. As will be illustrated in Chapter 5, when relating specific conditions to the vital signs measurements, oftentimes, several parameters will exhibit effects simultaneously (e.g., respiration rate and end-tidal carbon dioxide; intracranial pressure, non-invasive blood pressure, and pulse) and, by tracking these several parameters simultaneously, the likelihood is increased that a clinically meaningful effect is being observed when vital signs parameters change or are altered simultaneously [88, 125].

As an example of the meaning of a multi-parameter threshold alarm, consider the vital signs plotted against time in Figure 3.9. Here, three parameters are shown: peripheral oxygen saturation measurement (SpO_2), end-tidal carbon dioxide ($etCO_2$), and respiration rate (f_r). All three vital signs are plotted independently of one another in the time-series diagram. Also plotted

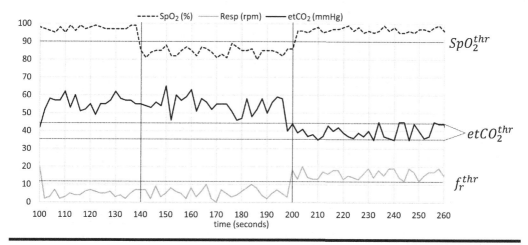

Figure 3.9   Example of a multi-parameter threshold alarm signal trigger. (Data source: author.)

are the predefined thresholds associated with these parameters. These are selected illustratively as follows:

$$\text{SpO}_2^{\text{thr}} = 90\%$$

$$35\,\text{mmHg} \leq \text{etCO}_2^{\text{thr}} \leq 45\,\text{mmHg}$$

$$f_r = 12 \text{ respirations per minute}$$

Each of these individually represent a single-parameter threshold or range to which the respective signal must conform or else an alarm signal will be annunciated. In the case of these parameters, all are seen as breaching their respective thresholds between 140 seconds and approximately 200 seconds. Hence, the conditions identified for an alarm signal annunciation is given by the expressions in Equations 3.13a–c:

$$\text{SpO}_2\left(t_i\right) \leq \text{SpO}_2^{\text{thr}} \tag{3.13a}$$

$$35 \geq \text{etCO}_2\left(t_i\right) \text{ or } \text{etCO}_2\left(t_i\right) \geq 45 \tag{3.13b}$$

And:

$$f_r\left(t_i\right) \leq f_r^{\text{thr}} \tag{3.13c}$$

These expressions state that if the instantaneous value of all three parameters simultaneously violate their respective threshold values, then the alarm signal is annunciated. The violation of the thresholds in combination can be visualized with the aid of Figure 3.9. Note that the end-tidal CO_2 parameter has actually breached its threshold before the time of 140 seconds. But, as the objective was to illustrate the effect of multi-parameter threshold breaches, the actual annunciation of an alarm would not take place until all of the parameters under consideration had simultaneously breached their respective threshold values.

Multi-parameter threshold alarms are designed to take into account more clinically actionable information and be more representative of conditional changes that will carry higher specificity than single parameter threshold breaches. The reason for this is the expected changes in parameters for a number of conditions, ranging from intracranial pressure increases to sleep apnea and respiratory depression, reflect variations in more than one vital sign observation. Thus, when two or more parameter measurements of vital signs violate their respective limits concurrently, this is a sign that the two parameters may be associated in terms of the changes or correlated in terms of the reason for their changes. The triggering conditions may be a simple limit threshold breach, or the individual parameters may conform to other criteria, including representing a non-self-correcting threshold breach in one or more parameter simultaneously. For instance, an increase in blood pressure (sudden onset or gradual increase) combined with a decrease in pulse rate, or a decrease in pulse rate combined with a change in breathing pattern, can be a very bad sign, indicating an intracranial hemorrhage. This may particularly be the case if context is brought into consideration: the subject is an elderly patient with a known or suspected fall involving evidence of head trauma, such as a contusion or a bleeding wound to the scalp. Thus, if these parameter measurements are found to vary together in time, the combination of these parameter changes concurrently is probably unlikely to occur as separate random events. It is more likely that they are correlated* or otherwise associated with one another. Another example application of a multi-parameter threshold alarm is identifying when patient respirations and end-tidal carbon dioxide meet simultaneous conditions that are indicative of,

---

* Correlation (Merriam-Webster): "a relation existing between phenomena or things or between mathematical or statistical variables which tend to vary, be associated, or occur together in a way not expected on the basis of chance alone."

Table 3.4   Example of a Multi-Parameter Threshold Alarm Specification

If:	$f_R < 8$ breaths/minute	[specification: duration $> \Delta t_{f_R}$]
And:	$etCO_2 > 50$ mmHg	[specification: duration $> \Delta t_{etCO_2}$]
And:	$SpO_2 < 90\%$	[specification: duration $> \Delta t_{SpO_2}$]

say, hypoventilation* and hypercarbia†. Thus, the multi-parameter threshold alarm follows the logic in the example of hypoventilation shown in Table 3.4.

The logic and specification of the multi-parameter threshold alarm described in Table 3.4 states that three parameters: respiration rate (f_R), end-tidal carbon dioxide ($etCO_2$), and peripheral pulse oximetry measurement (SpO_2) are to be considered together in terms of an alarm annunciation. The specific thresholds are based on the clinical understanding of the patient demographic and the practice of medicine. The values of 8 breaths per minute, 50 mmHg, and 90% are examples, although they are informed by clinical practice associated with identifying hypoventilation and hypoxemia. The logic specifies "AND" with each alarm condition, implying that if any one parameter threshold is not in violation of its particular parameter threshold, then the alarm will not annunciate. It is only when the parameter threshold violations occur AND the durations on those thresholds are met (here, given by Δt_{f_R}, Δt_{etCO_2}, and Δt_{SpO_2}, respectively) that the alarm signal annunciation occurs. Hence it is far less likely for all three parameters to be in violation simultaneously without some underlying cause.

3.10 Frequency-Based Alarms or Alarm Signals Based on Cyclic Parameter Behavior

Frequency-based or cyclic parameter based alarm signals refers to alarm signals that are triggered on repeated or transient behavior, such as may occur when a PCD measured value violates a limit repeatedly. These alarms, which will be referred to as frequency-based, have time and frequency characteristics that can translate into clinically actionable events (e.g., cyclic breathing patterns [16]). These alarm signals are distinct from non-self-correcting alarm

---

* hypoventilation: respiration inadequate for ventilation and necessary oxygen and carbon dioxide gas exchange.

† hypercarbia: excess carbon dioxide in blood stream, typically indicative of inadequate (slow) respiration.

signals in that the duration above or below a particular threshold is not the focus, but, rather, the focus is the quantity or frequency with which the threshold breach occurs.

Examples of clinical behavior that might be considered to display such behavior are peak pressure spikes associated with possible occlusions of an endotracheal tube of a mechanically ventilated patient, or the breathing pattern of an apneic patient. The cyclic action may repeat, or it may be transient; that is to say, the signal behavior may repeat after a period of time or after a period of cessation of such behavior. What is being measured in this type of signal behavior is the number of times in which the measured signal breaches a specific threshold a finite number of times. Thus, this type of alarm signal is a crude proxy for more formalistic methods of signal processing. Those familiar with signal processing and mathematical techniques such as Fourier series or discrete wavelet transforms (DWT) may recognize the cyclic nature of the time-series signal and opt for methods that employ these more formalistic approaches of signal study rather than using a heuristic metric such as assessing the number of times a signal threshold is breached. Several mathematical techniques related to simple one-dimensional DWTs and signal frequency calculations are presented in the next chapter in order to satisfy this more rigorous demand for mathematical purity on the matter. Chapter 4 provides a more thorough treatment on cyclic behavior and signal periodicity.

3.11 Chapter Summary

The several techniques described herein are intended to provide a sampling to both initiate creative thinking in the reader and educate with some concrete examples as to how to incorporate signal behavior associated with vital signs obtained from various PCDs to create more meaningful clinical alarms. The objective is to reduce false alarm rate while at the same time maintaining or reducing false negative rate. The alarm signal examples presented here require clinician involvement to validate in the patient care setting. Creating new alarms, therefore, necessitates the close interaction between those trained clinically to observe and understand the pragmatic signs of outward distress that patients can experience and those trained in manipulating and studying data and signals. Hence, the analytics complements the clinical, and one without the other can produce ineffective or even dangerous results: one who applies mathematical alarm signal techniques without understanding the impact on the patient is really engaging only in an academic exercise. On the other hand, employing simple threshold breach alarms will most likely yield non-clinically actionable results that will become ineffective for the clinician as they will inundate the clinician with non-actionable noise which can translate into missed events and can increase the possibility of incurring patient safety hazards in the clinical setting. A balance, therefore, must be achieved that involves viewing both sides: clinical practice and mathematical sophistication.

Thus, clinical surveillance involves applying mathematical techniques to physiological measurements in ways that will improve the sensitivity and specificity of the resultant alarm signals. In this way, the prospect of identifying deleterious clinical conditions can be determined earlier with the prospect of stemming them and preventing further deterioration, or reversing deterioration and preventing tragic consequences to the patient. The chapter that follows will delve more closely into techniques and methods that are employed in identifying correlated clinical events.

Chapter 4

Mathematical Techniques Applied to Clinical Surveillance

In this chapter an investigation into various mathematical approaches is undertaken to demonstrate the analysis and study of time-series-based physiological data with an emphasis on filtering and signal processing formalistic approaches. The objective is to illustrate the application of these methods that can be translated into generalizable rules for the creation of more clinically actionable alarm signals.

4.1 Moving Average: Simple Time-Averaging to Achieve Signal Smoothing

Time-averaging involves computing the running or moving average value of a signal, thereby removing the bulk of the high and low values or instantaneous deviations from a time series. The objective in moving averages is to smooth out a time-series signal, thereby reducing the number of values that are excessively high or excessively low. Running or moving averages take into account a specific quantity of measurements that (typically) remain constant in quantity. As new measurements are obtained they are included in the moving average calculation as the oldest measurements are removed from the moving average calculation. In this way, the average is continuously updated and computed, with each new measurement resulting in the possibility of a change in the moving average over time. The smoothness of the moving average depends on the quantity of measurements contained in the moving average calculation relative to the variation in the individual measurements comprising the moving average. Each measurement in the moving average calculation is equally weighted. That is, the weight or importance of the oldest measurement is equal in importance to the newest measurement obtained. The overall or net effect of the moving average calculation is a reduced level of threshold breaches due to the resultant smoothing of the signal. Yet, this smoothing comes at a cost: in applying the moving average, the instantaneous variations in the signal, which may carry clinically significant importance, can be smoothed over and lost, and variations in the signal that are possibly clinically significant can be missed due to this smoothing effect. Furthermore, the current value of the smoothed signal is based on the immediate past history. For example, if a time-series is averaged over the preceding 60 seconds, then the average value at the current time is computed using the current value plus all preceding values within the last 60 seconds, given equal weighting of those values within the moving average sample.

In the preceding chapter, a method was presented for computing the running or moving time average of a signal. Recall Equation 3.7:

$$\hat{V}(t) = \frac{1}{N} \sum_{t=t_i-\Delta t}^{t=t_i} V(t) \tag{3.7}$$

This expression describes the running average of the parameter $V(t)$ over a time interval Δt. Beginning with Equation 3.7, substitute for the variable Δt the difference between the current time, t_i, and the time in the past corresponding to the N-th measurement used in the moving average calculation, t_{i-N}. Thus, defining Δt as:

$$\Delta t = t_i - t_{i-N} \tag{4.1}$$

Let the current time be given by the time t_i, with the index i corresponding to the time of the latest measurement. Furthermore, let N represent the quantity of measurements corresponding to Δt time units in the past.

Then, Equation 3.7 can be re-written by referring to the current time t at index i as t_i. This re-write simply changes the variable frame of reference of Equation 3.7, resulting in the new Equation for moving average, 4.2:

$$\hat{V}(t_i) = \frac{1}{N} \sum_{t=t_{i-N}}^{t=t_i} V(t) \tag{4.2}$$

Moving averages are demonstrated relative to the heart rate (HR) measurements in the plots of Figures 4.1–4.4. The individual measurements are given by $V(t)$. The interval over which measurements are averaged ranges from time $t=t_{i-N}$ to time $t=t_i$, where N represents the total quantity of measurements within this time interval. The end result, $\widehat{V}(t_i)$, represents the time-averaged value of the measurements at time $t=t_i$. A closer inspection of each plot follows.

The plot of Figure 4.1 illustrates a 2,000 second sampling of heart rate measurements from a larger sample, The focus of the segment between 3,400 and 5,400 seconds was chosen because of the variations in heart rate behavior observed during this interval. This segment is particularly illustrative of the benefits obtained using moving averages because of the varied behavior of the signal over time.

Figure 4.2 shows the same interval of heart rate measurements, but with a 30-second time-averaged signal overlaid on top of the raw measurements. This means that $\Delta t = t_i - t_{i-N} = 30$ seconds. As can be seen, the "peaks" and "valleys" of the time-averaged signal are less "extreme" than the raw signal, but, upon closer inspection, one can also see that the peaks of the time-averaged signal are slightly lagging behind the peaks of the raw signal measurements. This is due to the fact that the average value of the measurement computed retrospectively takes into account these peaks or extreme values in the calculation process and, therefore, exhibits a delayed or phase-shifted

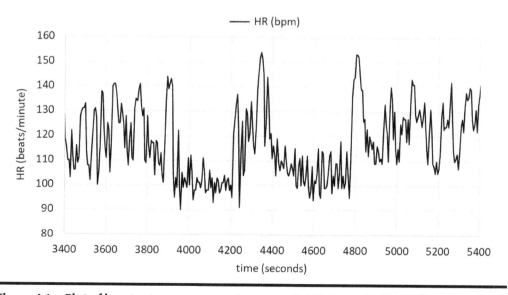

Figure 4.1 Plot of heart rate measurement across a 2,000 second window from 3,400 seconds through 5,400 seconds in the sample. Measurements are obtained every 6 seconds. (Data source: author.)

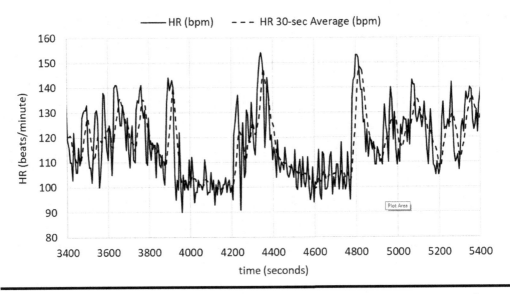

Figure 4.2 Plot of heart rate measurement with an overlay of the time-averaged signal, given 30 seconds of time-averaging. (Data source: author.)

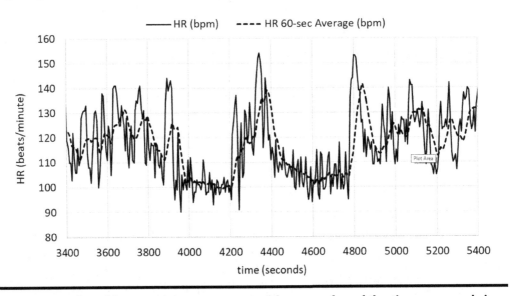

Figure 4.3 Plot of heart rate measurement with an overlay of the time-averaged signal, given 60 seconds of time-averaging. (Data source: author.)

response in the time-average. This delay becomes longer as the time-average lengthens. Thus, the plot of Figure 4.3 illustrates the case where the time-averaging interval is 60 seconds, and the plot of Figure 4.4 shows the effects of a 90-second time-averaging window. Again, the effect of the averaging is to smooth the signal, making the instantaneous peaks and valleys less extreme.

The variability associated with the effects of increasing the time-averaging sample can be quantified using the calculations of median and interquartile

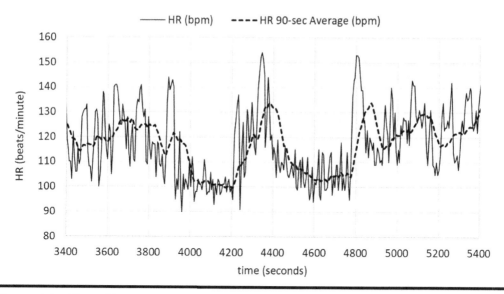

Figure 4.4   Plot of heart rate measurement with an overlay of the time-averaged signal, given 90 seconds of time-averaging.

range over the averaging time span of interest. A comparison among the various time-averaged signals is reflected in Table 4.1. The measures contained in this table require some explanation.

Beginning with the first column below the header in Table 4.1:

■ Minimum: the minimum value associated with the signal ensemble (raw HR, 30-second, average, 60-second average, 90-second average).
■ Q1: the first quartile; 25% of measurements fall between the minimum and the Q1 value.
■ Median: 50% of measurements exist above and below the median; 25% of measurements exist between Q1 and the median.
■ Q3: the third quartile; 25% of measurements fall between the median and the Q3 value.
■ Maximum: the maximum value associated with the ensemble of measurements under consideration; 25% of measurements fall between Q3 and the maximum value.
■ Range: the difference between maximum and minimum values.
■ IQR: interquartile range; the difference between Q3 and Q1; 50% of measurements fall within this range.
■ Outlier+: equal Q3 plus $1.5 \times$ IQR.
■ Outlier−: equal to Q1 minus $1.5 \times$ IQR.
■ Mean: the statistical mean of the ensemble of measurements.

Table 4.1 Raw Signal Measurement Distributions in Comparison with Running Averages for the Sample Signal

HR units of measure: beats/minute	HR (3400–5400 seconds)	30-second HR average	60-second HR average	90-second HR average
Minimum	78	78	79	79
Q1	106	109	110	110
Median	115	117	118	118
Q3	127	125	124	124
Maximum	154	148	142	136
Range	76	70	63	57
Interquartile range	21	16	14	14
Outlier+	159	148	145	144
Outlier−	75	85	89	90
Mean	116	116	116	116

The box-and-whisker plot of Figure 4.5 visualizes the data from Table 4.1. As the running average interval increases (that is, 30 seconds to 60 seconds to 90 seconds), corresponding to including more samples in the moving average window, the spread of the data narrows, indicative of smoothing of the data. This can be seen by inspecting the Range row in Table 4.1: as one moves from the left-most column to the right-most column, the range decreases as well as the interquartile range. This means that the larger variations become averaged out and normalized, resulting in less extreme variations in the time-averaged signal. Thus, moving averages can be effective at removing the "sharp edges" in the data, resulting in fewer extreme variations that can cause threshold breaches and the associated alarm signals that will be generated by signal breaches.

While intuitive and expected it is perhaps worthwhile to state explicitly that as more raw data points are included in the moving average calculation the result is a smoother signal that is less reactive to sudden changes in the raw signal measurements. Whereas, this has the advantage of reducing the likelihood of experiencing threshold breaches related to extreme changes in the raw measurements, the disadvantage is that the resulting average is phase-shifted so that signal variations that may indeed be meaningful are not "experienced" until later in time. These "extremes" in the raw signal measurements are no longer visible, thereby increasing the possibility that any true clinical event associated with them would be omitted or smoothed over.

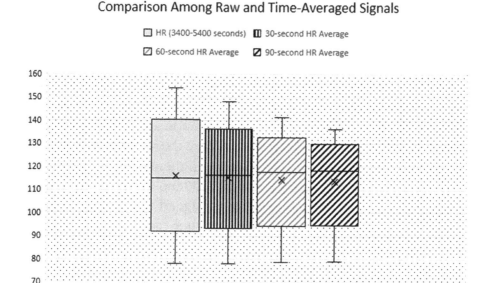

Figure 4.5 **Box-and-whisker plots of data contained in Table 4.1.**

Another approach for smoothing of signals will next be discussed that relies on the Kalman filter—a method of least-squares optimal filtering. The Kalman filter brings with it the added value that computations can be performed without maintaining the individual measurement history required of moving average calculations.

4.2 More Formalized Time-Series Filtering: The Kalman Filter

Kalman filtering employs a recursive algorithm that is referred to as an optimal estimator of a signal. The Kalman filter calculates an estimate of a parameter, usually with respect to a time-series, based upon uncertain or noisy observations. A benefit of the Kalman filter is that it allows recursive processing of measurements in real-time as observations are made and, thus, can be applied readily to live data. The Kalman filter also provides a mechanism for tuning to enable attenuating signal noise. The Kalman filter is an optimal estimator in the sense that it *minimizes the mean square error of the estimated parameters* [70].

Kalman filtering has many advocates and many applications. The use of formalized methods including least-squares techniques and Kalman filtering applied to medical signals has been widely studied [71–73].

Computation of the Kalman filter involves a *two-step process* whereby, in the first step, a *prediction* is made to a future state, followed by a second step involving a *measurement update*. The two steps then iterate back and forth between each other, and the result is a converged estimate of state that weights the measurements and the prediction based upon a balance between the confidence in either the measurements or the prediction. If measurements are weighted more heavily (i.e., more confidence in the accuracy of the measurements), then the filter will tend to follow those. If the predicted state is weighted more heavily (i.e., less confidence in the measurements than a model of the predicted state), then the filter will tend to follow the predicted state. The result in the former case is a more "jagged" filtered signal that follows the raw measurements; the result in the latter case is a smoother rendering of the estimated signal state, similar in character to running or moving averages over time. The key operational difference between the moving average and the Kalman filter is that the weighting can be adjusted between measurements and prediction, depending upon which are to be relied on more heavily, thereby changing the characteristic smoothing of the filtered signal. Furthermore, there is no need to maintain a long list of values from which to compute the average value continuously over time. That is, the Kalman filter operates on the basis of a computed state covariance and the current state of the signal measurements. Thus, computationally, the Kalman filter is very efficient when compared with the moving average calculation.

The development that follows is derived from several sources and is simplified to one dimension, which is representative of filtering a single parameter value obtained over time from a PCD [70, 74].

The equations defining the Kalman filter include the state estimate model (Equation 4.3) and the measurement update (Equation 4.4), and are given in the notation typically employed in the literature:

$$V_{t_{k+1}} = A \times V_{t_k} + B \times u_{t_{k+1}} + q_{t_k} \tag{4.3}$$

$$z_{t_{k+1}} = H \times V_{t_{k+1}} + r_{t_{k+1}} \tag{4.4}$$

Where:

$V_{t_{k+1}}$ is the state vector containing the estimate of the future state of the parameter at time t_{k+1} based on the previous state at time t_k, given by V_{t_k};

$u_{t_{k+1}}$ is the control input; this is any external forcing function applied to change the measured state;

A is the state transition matrix (or scalar variable in the case of one-dimensional parameters) which propagates the effect of each system state parameter at time t_k on the system state at time t_{k+1}, resulting in the translation and transitioning of the value of the parameter at the previous time to the current time. Note that the term "parameter" is meant to indicate a finding, such as heart rate or respiration rate or oxygen saturation;

B is the control input matrix which applies the effect of each control input parameter in the vector $u_{t_{k+1}}$ on the state V_{t_k}. This is another way of stating any external forcing on the parameter V_{t_k} that affects the manner in which the parameter is transitioned from time t_k to time t_{k+1};

q_{t_k} is the process noise term at time t_k for the estimated parameter as it makes its transition from the previous state at time t_k to time t_{k+1}. The process noise states that there is inherent uncertainty and aberration in the system that is accommodated crudely by a random (and, effectively, uncorrelated) process. The process noise is assumed to be drawn from a zero mean normal distribution with covariance given by the covariance matrix Q_{t_k}. In other words, the noise term $q_{t_k} = N(0, \sigma_Q^2)$, where σ_Q^2 is the variance in the process noise. The value of this parameter is taken as an assumption and an example of the effect of this term in relation to the measurement noise that will be shown to assist in bounding where the values should be set;

$z_{t_{k+1}}$ the value of the parameter measurement at time t_{k+1};

H is the transformation matrix that maps the measured parameter (i.e., the signal) from the frame of reference of the measurement domain to the estimated parameter domain. For example, if the measurement is a voltage of, say, the electrocardiogram signal, then H maps the voltage to millimeters on the electrocardiogram. In the case of most discrete signals from PCDs, however, this mapping will be unity (i.e., H=1) since the measurement domain will exactly match the parameter domain; and, finally,

r_{t_k} is the measurement noise term for each observation or measurement of the parameter. The measurement noise is assumed to have the character of zero mean normal or Gaussian noise with covariance R. In this sense, the measurement noise is typically similar in character to the process noise. The measurement noise term is specified as $r_{t_k} = N(0, \sigma_R^2)$, where σ_R^2 is the variance in the measurement noise. In practice, particularly as relates to measurements from PCDs, it is observed that variations are not large in terms of the process or the measurement noise. One can accommodate in these terms, of course, representations of the artifact, such as outliers in measurement akin to stray signals or models of patient movement.

The Kalman filter balances the confidence in the measurements with the confidence in the parameter estimates. In other words, suppose that in measuring heart rate the signal measurements themselves are trusted and are accurate, then the measurements will be the best predictor of the current and future state of the heart rate signal. If, on the other hand, the measurement accuracy is suspect as there is noise and artifact associated with it (i.e., noisy signals associated with poorly attached electrodes), then the measurements will be weighted less and a greater weight will be placed on the ensemble of measurements to guide the estimate of the future state, much in the same way as the moving average calculation was made. That is, the filter will respond more closely to the measurements if the "belief" or confidence in the measurements is greater than the confidence in the parameter estimate, or it will assume the character of a weighted average if confidence in the measurements is in question. If the measurement noise is high, the confidence in the measurements is fairly low, and the filter will smooth out the transitions between measurements, resulting in a state estimate which is less perturbed but also that does not react to sudden changes in measurements (hence, less likely to react to sudden or spurious changes).

The concept of a state estimate will now be introduced wherein the caret placed over the variable represents the expected value or estimate of the parameter. Thus, $\hat{V}_{t_k}$ represents the estimated value of the parameter at time t_k.

The Kalman filter maintains an estimate of the parameter state together with an estimate of the error represented by the *state covariance matrix*. The estimates of the state and the state covariance matrix are defined by the expressions reflecting their values at current and future time:

$$\hat{V}_{t_k|k} \equiv \text{estimate of } V_{t_k} \text{ given measurements } z_{t_k}, z_{t_{k-1}}, \ldots$$

$$\hat{V}_{t_{k+1}|k} \equiv \text{estimate of } V_{t_{k+1}} \text{ given measurements } z_{t_k}, z_{t_{k-1}}, \ldots$$

The error covariance of the state estimate is given by:

$$P_{t_k|k} \equiv \text{covariance of } V_{t_k} \text{ given measurements } z_{t_k}, z_{t_{k-1}}, \ldots$$

$$P_{t_{k+1}|k} \equiv \text{covariance of } V_{t_{k+1}} \text{ given measurements } z_{t_k}, z_{t_{k-1}}, \ldots$$

Referring back to the development of Equation 4.3, this equation can be further simplified: there is no external forcing, so $u_{t_k} \equiv 0$. Furthermore, the values of A and H in this unique case are unity (that is, no transformation from measurement to parameter frame of reference). Hence, these two constants reduce to unity, per Equations 4.5 and 4.6, respectively:

$$A = 1 \tag{4.5}$$

$$H = 1 \tag{4.6}$$

Thus, the solution process is then as outlined in Table 4.2.

Newly introduced here is the Kalman gain, $K_{t_{k+1}}$, which operates on the residuals (i.e., differences) between the measurement and state updates to produce an *"innovation"* or change (or difference) in the future state estimate that is based on the computed difference between the future state estimate and the measurement. This defines the amount by which the next estimate is to be adjusted based on the difference between the projection of the current state and any observed measurement at the future time.

The remaining steps involve the calculation of the updated state covariance, P, per Table 4.3.

Table 4.2 Kalman Filter Processing Algorithm

Time update (aka, parameter state prediction)	Measurement update (aka, measurement correction)	
Initialization: known values of $\hat{V}_{t_k\|k}, u_{t_k}, P_{t_k\|k}, z_{t_{k+1}}$ (i.e., new measurement)		
$\hat{V}_{t_{k+1}\|k} = \hat{V}_{t_k\|k} + w_{t_k}$ (4.7)	← (State prediction)	
$\hat{z}_{t_{k+1}\|k} = \hat{V}_{t_{k+1}\|k}$ (4.8)	← (Measurement prediction)	
(Measurement residual) →	$\Delta\hat{z}_{t_{k+1}} = z_{t_{k+1}} - \hat{z}_{t_{k+1}\|k}$	(4.9)
(Updated state estimate) →	$\hat{V}_{t_{k+1}\|k+1} = \hat{V}_{t_{k+1}\|k} + K_{t_{k+1}} \times \Delta\hat{z}_{t_{k+1}}$	(4.10)

Table 4.3 Kalman Filter State Covariance Estimation Process

Process step	Equation	
State covariance	$P_{t_{k+1}\|k} = P_{t_k\|k} + Q_{t_k}$	(4.11)
Kalman gain (note: if multi-dimensional, then this step involves the multiplication of the inverse of the sum of the state covariance and measurement covariance matrix)	$K_{t_{k+1}} = \dfrac{P_{t_{k+1}\|k}}{P_{t_{k+1}\|k} + R_{t_k}}$	(4.12)
State covariance update	$P_{t_{k+1}\|k+1} = \left(1 - K_{t_{k+1}}\right) \times P_{t_{k+1}\|k}$	(4.13)

Table 4.4 summarizes a sampling of data from the calculation of heart rate, HR, estimate using the Kalman filter in comparison with raw measurements of HR. The sample used earlier from the moving average calculation is revisited here for this calculation.

Recall that the balance between confidence in the measurements and confidence in the model allows for tuning of the performance of the Kalman filter. This balance is achieved through the judicious setting of the measurement error and the process noise. Recall that measurement noise covariance and process noise covariance are given by R_{t_k} and Q_{t_k}, respectively.

Figures 4.6 and 4.7 illustrate two cases: the first, in which the measurement error (R_{t_k}) is set very low in relation to the process noise (Q_{t_k}), and the second, in which the opposite case is considered. Figure 4.6 illustrates the case of very low measurement noise, in which the Kalman filter estimate follows the raw measurements very closely, and the case of very low process noise, respectively, in which the Kalman filter estimate follows the ensemble of measurements very closely. Figure 4.7 illustrates the case of low process noise/large measurement noise, in which the Kalman filter estimate follows the signal average over time. Figure 4.8, illustrates an extreme case, in which the process noise is taken down to a value of 0.001, resulting in a predicted state estimate that is almost entirely smooth and devoid of major variations.

The further smoothing of the signal can be seen quite dramatically in this last figure. As was done in the case of signal averaging, it is possible to quantify and visualize the amount of variation in the signal by using box-and-whisker plots. As a general rule, it is appropriate to use the median and the interquartile range in calculations when the distribution of the measurements about a mean value is not known to be symmetric or is demonstrably

Table 4.4 Sample Calculations Illustrating the Performance of the Kalman Filter

Time (seconds)	HR measurement	r(tk)	q(tk) (process noise)	Pk(tk)	HR-KF	K(tk)
0	80	0.010	0.100	10.000	0.000	0.999
6	80	0.010	0.100	0.010	79.921	0.999
12	81	0.010	0.100	0.009	80.910	0.917
18	79	0.010	0.100	0.009	79.160	0.916
24	80	0.010	0.100	0.009	79.930	0.916
30	80	0.010	0.100	0.009	79.994	0.916
36	79	0.010	0.100	0.009	79.083	0.916

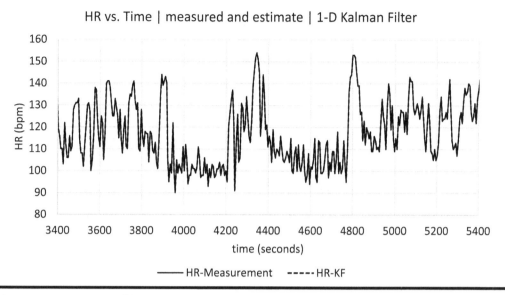

Figure 4.6   Measured heart rate versus Kalman filter estimate of heart rate; low measurement noise case ($r_{t_k} = 0.01$).

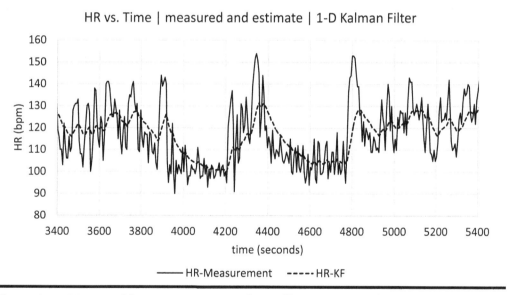

Figure 4.7   Measured heart rate versus Kalman filter estimate of heart rate; low process noise case ($q_{t_k} = 0.01$).

asymmetric. Thus, for measured distributions of medical device parameters, the comparison in terms of the signal median, mean, and interquartile range will be performed as metrics for comparison.

The resulting table, Table 4.5, quantifies the changes in the character of the filtered heart rate parameter versus raw measurements, and is illustrated

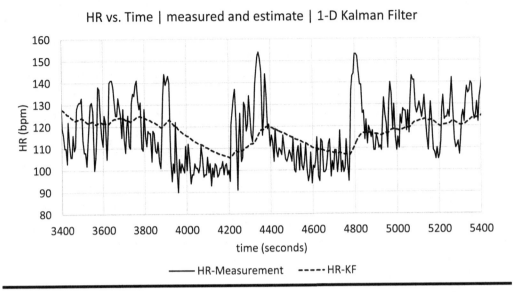

Figure 4.8 **Measured heart rate versus Kalman filter estimate of heart rate; lowest process noise case ($q_{t_k} = 0.001$).**

Table 4.5 **Comparison between Raw Heart Rate Measurements and Kalman Filter Estimates of Heart Rate among Various Levels of Measurement and Process Noise**

Interval from 3400 s–5400 s	Heart rate measurements	Kalman filter (r=0.01)	Kalman filter (q=0.01)	Kalman filter (q=0.001)
Minimum	90	91	99	100
Q1	105	105	107	110
Median	115	115	117	119
Q3	128	127	124	123
Maximum	154	154	144	131
Interquartile range	23	22	18	14
Outlier–	71	73	80	89
Outlier+	162	160	151	144

in Figure 4.9. As can be seen in this figure, as the process noise is reduced (implying higher confidence in the model), the width of the box and whisker plots narrows (that is, variation is reduced). This implies fewer breaches or deviations from the median value of the measured signal, effectively providing a means of reducing alarm signal annunciations.

If the objective is to minimize the number of false alarms and to define a true event as the repeated occurrence of a measurement outside of an

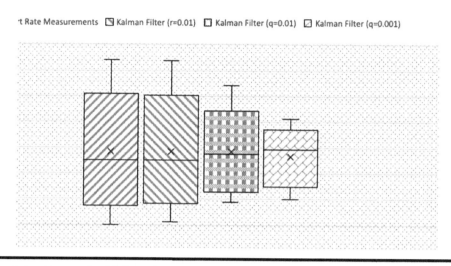

Figure 4.9   Box-and-whisker plots associated with raw heart rate measurements and Kalman filter with various levels of measurement and process noise.

acceptable threshold range, it may be possible to tailor such thresholds by astutely selecting the sensitivity of the model for the raw signal data, thereby achieving a balance between the number of consecutive occurrences of a threshold breach that can induce higher false alarm rates.

As a point of clarification related to all alarm threshold settings, the selection of parameter thresholds must be within the purview and control of the licensed clinician as part of the practice of medicine. Technology cannot make these decisions as technical algorithms would need to take into account the full context of the patient and the clinical training of the end-user.

4.3 Signal Periodicity and Filtering Noisy Signal Behavior

An additional area of focus when it comes to time-series data collected from PCDs is the periodicity of the signal data. Periodicity can also become "entangled" with or misinterpreted as noise or artifact, further confounding the character of the signal. Such cyclic or periodic behavior is not limited to data retrieved at high frequency, such as electrocardiographic (ECG) signals, although this is what may frequently come to mind. The periodicity can be an indicator of a physiological trend (such as periods of continued sleep apnea) [22] or may be due to other physiological genuinely actionable causes. Such signals may be "infiltrated" by an artifact, as might be observed with ECG leads when noise is present in the signal. Artifact can be present in telemetry signals, particularly when patients are ambulatory, and may also be the case with the use of nasal cannula or continuous positive airway pressure (CPAP) masks: any situation in which a patient moves, or the possibility that the continuity of signal measurements may be broken between the patient and the PCD.

Two specific examples will be used to illustrate this point. Both examples are based on data taken from the Medical Information Mart for Intensive Care (MIMIC) critical care database [85, 86] and represent high frequency data collection of two very important parameters: one being arterial blood pressure (ABP) time-series measurement and the other being ECG signal measurement. One reason for filtering of data includes the smoothing of the artifact or spikes that are due to signal errors or other issues associated with signal acquisition, as is illustrated in the following figures.

Figure 4.10 illustrates a time-series sample of ABP data versus time. This is contrasted with the same signal containing some signal artifact (i.e., noise) present in the signal shown in Figure 4.11. In order to simulate the appearance of artifact in this signal, a normally distributed noise signal having a 2 mmHg standard deviation was overlaid on the measurement, resulting in the plot of this latter figure.

A Kalman filter estimate is created and overlaid on the signal containing the measurement artifact to illustrate the benefits achieved in terms of signal smoothing. The Kalman filter tracks the actual signal very closely while effectively filtering out the artifact in the signal. Thus, the filter does an

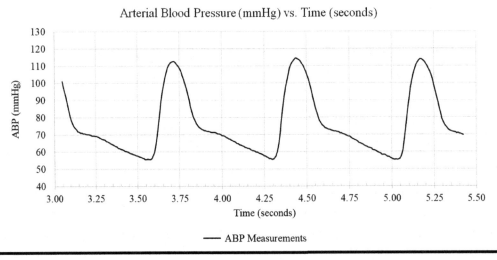

Figure 4.10 **Arterial blood pressure (ABP) measurement versus time. (Data source: MIMIC II.)**

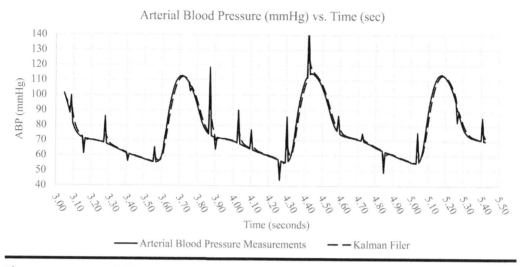

Figure 4.11   Arterial blood pressure (ABP) measurement versus time with measurement artifact overlaid. (Data source: MIMIC II and author.)

adequate job of "finding" the signal amidst the "clutter" of the artifact and revealing the periodic nature of this signal.

In studying signal characteristics, it is frequently important to understand whether periodicity or cyclic behavior exists. In signal analysis a measure that identifies dominant and secondary frequencies in stationary signals is achieved using Fourier analysis and, in particular, involves use of the Fourier transform. The Fourier transform maps signal behavior of a time-series from the time domain into the frequency domain. Fourier transforms and methods are also related to spectral analysis methods, such as periodograms. In laymen's terms, the generalized purpose of these methods is to map the time domain of the signal into frequency space for the purpose of identifying principal and secondary signal frequencies of the time series signal under consideration. Furthermore, the methods employed in spectral analysis provide an indicator of the relative "power" or dominance of a particular frequency or cyclic behavior of the time series under consideration. This is particularly useful when considering the study of the ABP, ECG, respiratory, or other time-varying signals for which periodic behavior carries clinical significance. When artifact (noise) is introduced into time-varying signals, this artifact can interfere or obscure the visibility of periodic behavior and thus result in errors in interpreting the signal characteristics.

The mathematical development of these methods is beyond the scope of this text. Yet, the equations will be provided so that the interested reader can observe their use.

4.4 Signal Frequency Assessments

As an introduction and for comparative purposes, Figure 4.12 depicts a plot of the power spectral density associated with the measurements shown in Figure 4.10. Figure 4.13 shows, in juxtaposition, the power spectral density

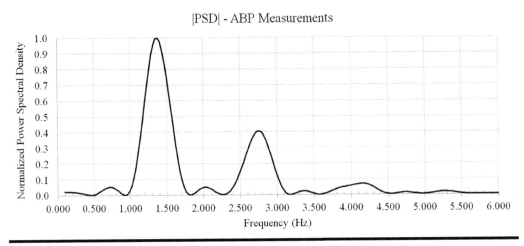

Figure 4.12   Normalized power spectral density of ABP signal measurements.

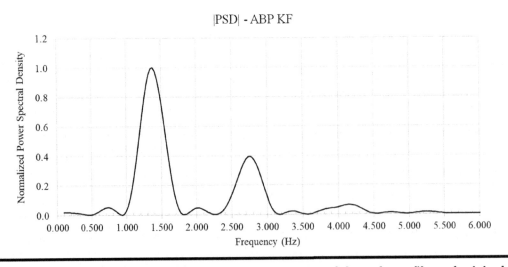

Figure 4.13   Normalized power spectral density (PSD) of the Kalman filter of original ABP signal measurements.

of the associated Kalman filtered signal of these same data. Note the close comparison between both Figure 4.12 and Figure 4.13: the Kalman filter does a good job of finding the signal despite the signal artifact imposed upon the modified ABP data of Figure 4.11.

Both Figures 4.12 and Figure 4.13 show the dominant signal frequency to be approximately 1.4 Hz–1.4 cycles per second. There is a secondary frequency of lesser dominance at approximately 2.8 Hz. The dominant frequency of 1.4 Hz translates into a heart rate frequency of approximately 84 beats per minute (bpm)—in the range of normal sinus rhythm. The principal frequencies determined in both Figure 4.12 and Figure 4.13 show that, despite the artifact, the frequency is centered about the primary or principal value of 84 bpm. The power spectral density identifies the dominant frequencies in a signal by the peaks of the PSD function at a specific value of frequency. In this way, the underlying frequencies of the time-series data can be determined.

One very popular method for spectral analysis (due to its application to time-series data containing gaps or uneven sampling) is the Lomb–Scargle periodogram (LSP). The use of the LSP for the analysis of biological signal rhythms is documented in the literature [77, 78]:

> The analysis of time-series of biological data often require special statistical procedures to test for the presence or absence of rhythmic components in noisy data, and to determine the period length of rhythms … the generalized Lomb-Scargle periodogram is a sufficient statistic for … frequency estimation. [77]
>
> … it is common to have incomplete or unevenly sampled time series … [and, as such] is not directly possible with methods such as Fast Fourier Transform (FFT) … the Lomb-Scargle method estimates a frequency spectrum based on a least-squares fit of sinusoid. [78]

A key benefit of the LSP is in its ability to process unequally spaced or missing data in terms of time, representing a distinct advantage over the Discrete Time Fourier transform (DTFT). The normalized power spectral density is calculated using Equations 4.13 and 4.14, respectively:

$$PSD(\omega) = \frac{1}{2\sigma^2} \left\{ \frac{\left[\sum_j (Y_j - \bar{Y}) \cos \omega (t_j - \tau)\right]^2}{\sum_j \cos^2 \omega (t_j - \tau)} \right.$$

$$\left. + \frac{\left[\left[\sum_j (Y_j - \bar{Y}) \sin \omega (t_j - \tau)\right]\right]^2}{\sum_j \sin^2 \omega (t_j - \tau)} \right\}$$

(4.13)

Where:

$$\tau = \left(\frac{1}{2\omega}\right) \tan^{-1} \left[\frac{\sum_j \sin 2\omega t_j}{\sum_j \cos 2\omega t_j}\right] \qquad (4.14)$$

The parameter PSD(ω) is the spectral power as a function of angular frequency. This parameter is often normalized based on the maximum value determined in the sample, and is typically plotted as a normalized magnitude with maximum value of 1 (unity), and with respect to the natural frequency, f, as follows from Equation 4.15:

$$PSD(f) = \frac{PSD(f)}{PSD(f)} \qquad (4.15)$$

The relationship between angular (or circular) frequency and frequency in units of Hertz (Hz) is given by Equation 4.16:

$$f = \frac{\omega}{2\pi} \qquad (4.16)$$

The solution of these equations is rather straightforward. A simple example will help to illustrate so that extrapolation to a more complex case can be performed.

Consider the following sine wave plotted in Figure 4.14. This sine wave is described by Equation 4.17:

$$y(t) = 10 \sin (2\pi f t) \qquad (4.17)$$

Here, the frequency, f, is equal to 0.01 Hz.

The normalized LSP for this simple waveform is shown in Figure 4.15. Note the sharp spike at the signal frequency of 0.01 Hz.

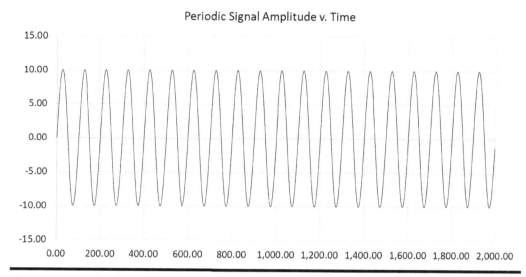

Figure 4.14 Simulated signal measurements $y(t) = 10\sin(2\pi f t)$; $f = 0.01$ Hz.

The LSP can also distinguish multiple frequencies from a time-series sample. In order to illustrate the effect of multiple frequencies on the ability of the LSP to identify them, consider the plot of Figure 4.16, which displays an example waveform given by Equation 4.18:

$$y(t) = 10\sin\left(2\pi f_1 t\right) + 5\sin\left(2\pi f_2 t\right); \; f_1$$
$$= 0.01\,\text{Hz}, \; f_2 = 0.005\,\text{Hz} \tag{4.18}$$

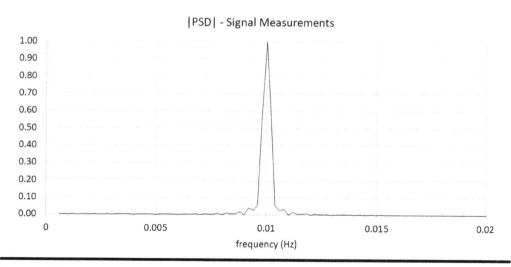

Figure 4.15 Power spectral density (PSD) for simulated signal measurements $y(t) = 10\sin(2\pi f t)$; $f = 0.01$ Hz.

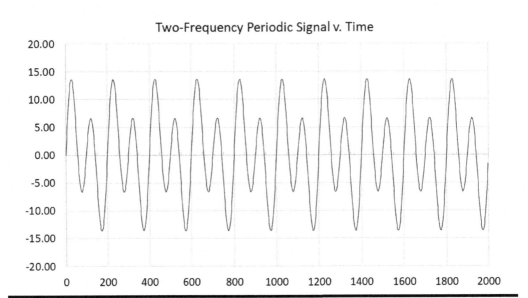

Figure 4.16   Simulated signal measurements
$y(t) = 10\sin(2\pi f_1 t) + 5\sin(2\pi f_2 t); f_1 = 0.01\text{Hz}, f_2 = 0.005\text{Hz}.$

The periodogram for this expression is illustrated in the plot of Figure 4.17. This figure shows two peaks: one associated with the principal frequency of $f_1 = 0.01$ Hz, and the second associated with the frequency of $f_2 = 0.005$ Hz. Note the amplitudes of the two components of this waveform are ten and five, respectively. Hence, the power or relative amplitude of the frequency represented in Figure 4.16 displays these as distinct amplitudes.

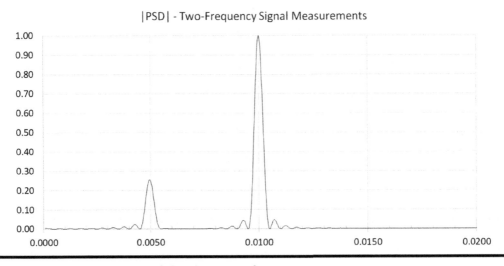

Figure 4.17   Power spectral density (PSD) for
$(t) = 10\sin(2\pi f_1 t) + 5\sin(2\pi f_2 t); f_1 = 0.01\text{Hz}, f_2 = 0.005\text{Hz}.$

Note that this signal contains two terms: the first with a magnitude of ten and the second with a magnitude of five. Furthermore, the second term has a frequency component exactly half of the first term. This signal has a power spectral density given by the plot of Figure 4.17. The normalized power spectrum shows the amplitude of this second component as being one-quarter that of the principal frequency, with amplitude ten. Thus, the LSP is quite effective in detecting and drawing out frequencies from waveforms.

This method can extend to an additional, more complex example: that of the electrocardiogram (ECG) signal. Consider the simple ECG signal (signal Lead II) of Figure 4.18. The power spectral density (PSD) is given in Figure 4.19. Note, however, that the frequency axis has been translated into beats per minute to aid viewing. The principal frequency is that of the ECG R-R intervals (the high signal peaks in Figure 4.18), which are separated in time by 1 second, corresponding to an average heart rate of 60 bpm. This is reflected well in the PSD plot as the principal frequency, shown in Figure 4.19. Other, lower power frequencies both higher and lower than 60 bpm are reflected in the time-series, representing the frequencies between the various components of the sinus waveform (i.e., the P, Q, S, and T waves).

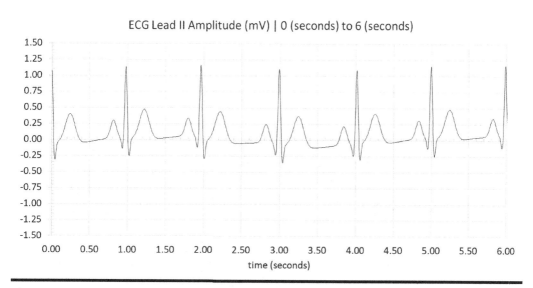

Figure 4.18 ECG Lead II signal sampling. (Data source: MIMIC II.)

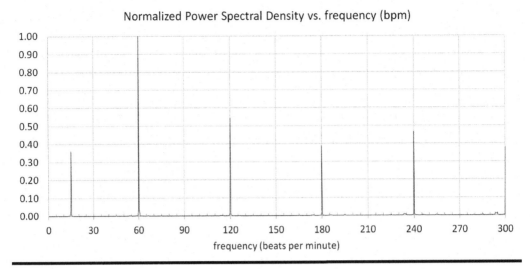

Figure 4.19 Power spectral density of ECG waveform versus frequency in beats per minute.

4.5 The Discrete Wavelet Transform

The discrete wavelet transform provides a system for constructing or approximating a signal or function. Unlike the Fourier transform or the LSP, which reflect the frequency or the spectral components of a signal, wavelets provide time and frequency localization of signal specifics, which is necessary to reconstruct time-varying, non-stationary processes [79, 80]. The discrete wavelet transform calculation is conducted with respect to a Haar-basis function, in which individual averages and differences (or details, as they are sometimes referred to in the art) are computed with respect to the raw signal data.

Consider a small sample signal of raw data given by Equation 4.19:

$$f^T = \begin{bmatrix} 5 & -2 & 3 & 1 \end{bmatrix} \tag{4.19}$$

The process of computing wavelet coefficients from this data vector is straightforward and is illustrated in Figure 4.20.

The discrete wavelet transform entails representing the original signal as a mean or average baseline and then computing deviations or variations in this baseline, calculated as secondary averages and differences between the individual signals and the average baseline. The signal is decomposed into a series of these averages and differences, where the average is calculated according to normal convention, and the difference is actually half the difference between any two raw signal values, as given by Equations 4.20 and 4.21.

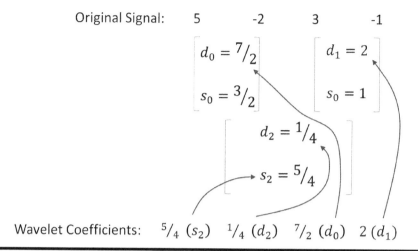

Original Signal: 5   -2   3   -1

$d_0 = \frac{7}{2}$ $d_1 = 2$

$s_0 = \frac{3}{2}$ $s_0 = 1$

$d_2 = \frac{1}{4}$

$s_2 = \frac{5}{4}$

Wavelet Coefficients: $\frac{5}{4}$ (s_2) $\frac{1}{4}$ (d_2) $\frac{7}{2}$ (d_0) 2 (d_1)

Figure 4.20 Computing methodology for Haar discrete wavelet transform.

Thus,

$$s_i = \frac{f_i + f_{i+1}}{2} \tag{4.20}$$

And,

$$d_i = \frac{f_i - f_{i+1}}{2} \tag{4.21}$$

The computations illustrated in Figure 4.20 proceed as follows: the average of each raw sample is calculated with respect to its immediate neighbor, together with the difference (divided by two). Once these are computed, the average and difference of these results are then calculated. This process continues until the complete ensemble (that is, the single value and difference) corresponding to the entire signal is determined. The first wavelet coefficient is given by the ensemble average corresponding to the longest scale value over the entire interval. The next wavelet coefficient corresponds to the size of the difference of the averages at the next scale (i.e., by considering the averages and differences of these newly computed averages and differences). The remaining coefficients follow the pattern of the differences between the averages at a finer and finer scale (in general). Thus, the vector of wavelet coefficients given the data sample above appears as follows in Equation 4.22, representing the transpose of the wavelet coefficient vector:

$$b^T = \begin{bmatrix} \frac{5}{4} & \frac{1}{4} & \frac{7}{2} & 2 \end{bmatrix} \tag{4.22}$$

The relationship between the wavelet coefficients and the raw signal is expressed mathematically in Equation 4.23:

$$f = H_4 \times b \tag{4.23}$$

Where H_4 represents a 4×4 Haar matrix having the form:

$$H_4 = \begin{bmatrix} 1 & 1 & 1 & 0 \\ 1 & 1 & -1 & 0 \\ 1 & -1 & 0 & 1 \\ 1 & -1 & 0 & -1 \end{bmatrix} \tag{4.24}$$

Alternatively, given the raw signal, the wavelet coefficients may be found using the inverse of the Haar basis matrix, according to Equation 4.25:

$$b = H_4^{-1} \times f \tag{4.25}$$

The Haar matrix may be inverted using standard methods. The creation of the Haar matrix follows a predictable pattern as the number of rows and columns increases. However, by applying the Haar transform, the size of the matrix increases according to a 2^n scale, where n is a positive integer. Thus, in the Haar basis, the quantity of data must conform to this scale as well. Expanding this 4×4 Haar basis to an 8×8 (H_8) basis yields Equation 4.26:

$$H_8 = \begin{bmatrix} 1 & 1 & 1 & 0 & 1 & 0 & 0 & 0 \\ 1 & 1 & 1 & 0 & -1 & 0 & 0 & 0 \\ 1 & 1 & -1 & 0 & 0 & 1 & 0 & 0 \\ 1 & 1 & -1 & 0 & 0 & -1 & 0 & 0 \\ 1 & -1 & 0 & 1 & 0 & 0 & 1 & 0 \\ 1 & -1 & 0 & 1 & 0 & 0 & -1 & 0 \\ 1 & -1 & 0 & -1 & 0 & 0 & 0 & 1 \\ 1 & -1 & 0 & -1 & 0 & 0 & 0 & -1 \end{bmatrix} \tag{4.26}$$

Note the pattern indicated between Equations 4.24 and 4.26: the first column is unity. The second column contains one-half +1 and one-half −1. The remaining columns are the sum and differences pairwise for each of the data elements in finer granularity.

Consider an example problem to illustrate the method. The original signal is expanded from four to eight elements. This larger data Haar basis function will help to illustrate some other features of the discrete wavelet transform. A sample signal, created somewhat arbitrarily, is given by Equation 4.27:

$$f^T = \begin{bmatrix} 5.000 & -2.000 & 3.000 & 1.000 & 9.000 & -3.000 & -5.000 \end{bmatrix} \qquad (4.27)$$

The vector of wavelet coefficients associated with this signal, found using H_8, is given by Equation 4.28:

$$b^T = \begin{bmatrix} 1.875 & -0.125 & -0.250 & 6.000 & 3.500 & 1.000 & -1.000 & 1.000 \end{bmatrix} \qquad (4.28)$$

A benefit of wavelet coefficients is that they establish the relative scale of the differences with respect to the overall signal average. This is important because, in terms of reproducing the signal, the values of these wavelet coefficients define their relative impact, or contribution, to the overall signal. Thus, compression of the original signal can be achieved (at a loss) by discarding certain coefficients via application of a threshold on significance.

Defining the statistical significance level of this threshold can be done in accordance with well-documented practices, especially relative to setting confidence intervals with respect to a known distribution [81–83]. However, the discarding of coefficients may not be the principal objective of the wavelet transform in medical applications since removing potentially important information from the raw signal can result in lost attributes that may carry clinical significance, similar to the concern expressed over moving time signal averaging expressed previously.

One way to illustrate this concept is by applying an exclusion threshold on the coefficients. The magnitude of the wavelet coefficients provides insight into the level of contribution each makes relative to reproducing the overall time signal. Hence, by omitting certain coefficients it becomes possible to exclude elements of the original signal, such as noise or other components that are judged to be of negligible influence on the overall raw data sample.

Consider the table of wavelet coefficients (Table 4.6). The column on the left is the independent variable (time). Each subsequent set of columns defines the set of Haar-basis wavelet coefficients and the resulting signal value, beginning with no threshold up to a value of 30% in increments of 10%. The threshold value is computed by multiplying the threshold percentage by the largest wavelet coefficient. In the case of the sample signal, from Equation 4.28, the absolute value of the largest Haar wavelet coefficient is equal to 6.000. If a 10% threshold is applied to this value, for instance, the result is 0.600. Thus, in reconstructing the signal, any wavelet coefficients with an absolute value less than 0.600 would be set to zero (0). In this case,

Table 4.6 Wavelet Coefficients for Reconstructing a Complete Signal, and Illustrating Wavelet Coefficient Threshold Levels

Time	No threshold		10% threshold			20% threshold			30% threshold		
	Wavelet coefficients	Signal	Wavelet coefficients	Signal	|Error|	Wavelet coefficients	Signal	|Error|	Wavelet coefficients	Signal	|Error|
1.0	1.875	5.000	1.875	5.375	0.375	1.875	5.375	0.375	1.875	5.375	0.375
2.0	−0.125	−2.000	0.000	−1.625	0.375	0.000	−1.625	0.375	0.000	−1.625	0.375
3.0	−0.250	3.000	0.000	2.875	0.125	0.000	1.875	1.125	0.000	1.875	1.125
4.0	6.000	1.000	6.000	0.875	0.125	6.000	1.875	0.875	6.000	1.875	0.875
5.0	3.500	7.000	3.500	6.875	0.125	3.500	7.875	0.875	3.500	7.875	0.875
6.0	1.000	9.000	1.000	8.875	0.125	0.000	7.875	1.125	0.000	7.875	1.125
7.0	−1.000	−3.000	−1.000	−3.125	0.125	0.000	−4.125	1.125	0.000	−4.125	1.125
8.0	1.000	−5.000	1.000	−5.125	0.125	0.000	−4.125	0.875	0.000	−4.125	0.875

two wavelet coefficients are discarded (−0.125, −0.250). The reconstructed signal, then, is not a precise representation of the original signal (i.e., is "lossy" compression).

At the 20% level, the threshold value is 1.200, and the coefficients (1.000, −1.000, 1.000) are excluded (i.e., set to zero so that their contribution will be ignored for signal reconstruction). In comparing the reconstructed signals in Figure 4.21 with thresholds of 10% and 20% to the original signal (i.e., "no threshold applied" signal), one can see that there are differences in the reconstructed signal. These differences have a maximum deviation of 1.125 between the reconstructed and the original signal.

In viewing the 30% threshold columns, three of the wavelet coefficients are excluded from waveform reconstruction. Here, the deviation between the original and reconstructed signals is no larger than 1.800. As the discard threshold approaches zero, the difference between the reconstructed and original signals approaches zero. Figure 4.21 provides a comparative view of these data by displaying all of these signals on one overlay plot. To the casual observer, there does not appear to be much difference between the *lossy* and the *lossless* cases: the signal data points all appear to be close to one another.

Depending on the behavior of the original signal (that is, its shape, repetitiveness, noise content), the degree of loss vis-à-vis discarding wavelet coefficients may be acceptable to the end-user. This case can be illustrated effectively with the aid of a revised form of the signal data. The data are contained in Table 4.7 and are plotted in Figure 4.22. The tolerance for

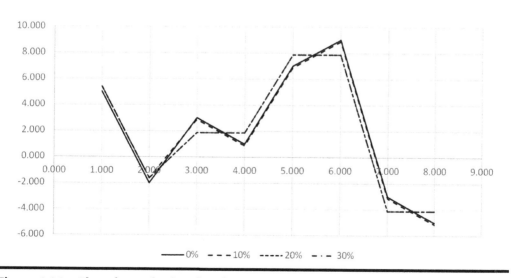

Figure 4.21   Plot of sample signal and Haar wavelet transform for the original signal and three different levels of Haar wavelet coefficient exclusion criteria: 0%, 10%, 20%, and 30%.

Table 4.7 Wavelet Coefficients for Revised Signal and Threshold Levels

Time	No threshold		10% threshold			20% threshold			30% threshold		
	Wavelet coefficients	Signal	Wavelet coefficients	Signal	|Error|	Wavelet coefficients	Signal	|Error|	Wavelet coefficients	Signal	|Error|
1.0	2.750	−7.000	2.750	−7.000	0.000	2.750	−7.000	0.000	2.750	−7.000	0.000
2.0	0.000	8.000	0.000	8.000	0.000	0.000	8.000	0.000	0.000	8.000	0.000
3.0	−2.250	9.000	−2.250	9.000	0.000	−2.250	9.000	0.000	−2.250	9.000	0.000
4.0	−4.250	1.000	−4.250	1.000	0.000	−4.250	1.000	0.000	−4.250	1.000	0.000
5.0	−7.500	−6.000	−7.500	−6.000	0.000	−7.500	−6.000	0.000	−7.500	−6.000	0.000
6.0	4.000	3.000	4.000	3.000	0.000	4.000	3.000	0.000	4.000	3.000	0.000
7.0	−4.500	10.000	−4.500	10.000	0.000	−4.500	10.000	0.000	−4.500	10.000	0.000
8.0	3.000	4.000	3.000	4.000	0.000	3.000	4.000	0.000	3.000	4.000	0.000

exclusion criteria is higher in this case, as removal of wavelet coefficients for reconstructing the signal has minimal or no impact on the integrity of the reconstructed signal.

Figure 4.22 overlays the raw signal data on the signal reconstruction using the entire set of wavelet coefficients. In this case, based on the shape of the signal, removing wavelet coefficients even at the 30% level has no effect on the integrity of the reconstructed signal.

As a generalized review, the DWT calculation is carried out in detail for a signal vector containing eight data elements. The first step is to compute the averages and differences (divided by two) for each of the signal components. This is shown in Table 4.8 through Table 4.11.

The next step involves computing the averages and differences of those averages and differences just computed. This is shown in Table 4.12 and Table 4.13, respectively.

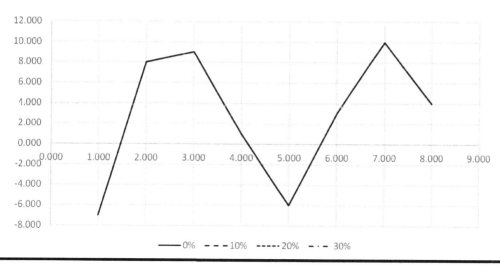

Figure 4.22 Plot of sample signal and Haar wavelet transform given all wavelet coefficients are applied.

Table 4.8 First Wavelet Coefficient Calculation

Original Signal:							
5.000	-2.000	3.000	1.000	7.000	9.000	-3.000	-5.000

$\dfrac{a+b}{2}$ — Averages: — $\dfrac{a-b}{2}$ — Differences:

1.500		2.000		8.000		-4.000		3.500		1.000		-1.000		1.000
	1.750				2.000				-0.250			6.000		
		1.875								-0.125				

Haar Discrete Wavelet Transform Coefficients:

1.875	-0.125	-0.250	6.000	3.500	1.000	-1.000	1.000

Table 4.9   Second Wavelet Coefficient Calculation

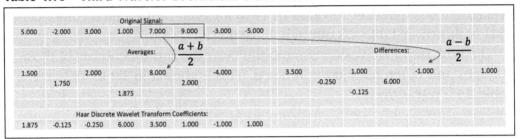

Table 4.10   Third Wavelet Coefficient Calculation

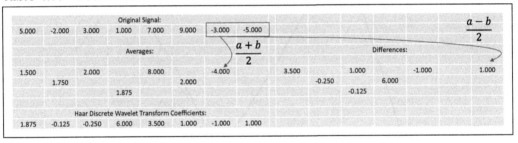

Table 4.11   Fourth Wavelet Coefficient Calculation

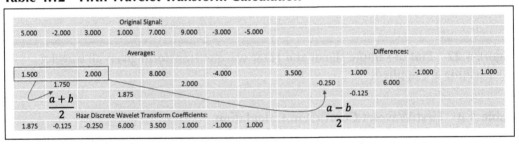

Table 4.12   Fifth Wavelet Transform Calculation

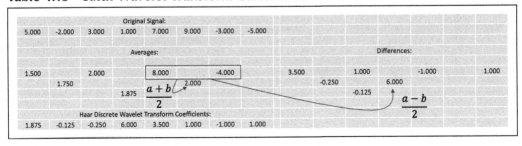

Table 4.13   Sixth Wavelet Transform Calculation

Table 4.14 Seventh Wavelet Transform Calculation

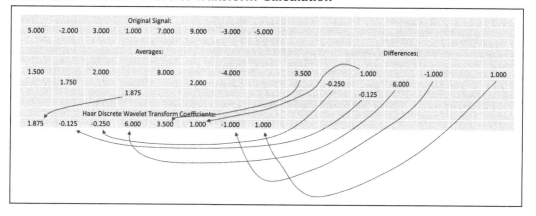

Finally, the last step involved is to compute the average and difference of the previous step. This is shown in Table 4.14.

This process lends itself well to automation.

4.6 Chapter Summary

The purpose of this chapter was to introduce the reader to various methods that can be used to process and analyze signals to detect cyclic events, normalize and reduce the artifact from signals, and detect periodicity in PCD data. Periodicity is very important to understand relative to time-varying signals such as electrocardiograms, plethysmography, capnography, and other discrete data for which clinical importance can be derived from an understanding of signal periodicity. An example of such clinical importance would be the case of varying respiratory rate, as might be detected in patients experiencing sleep apnea, Cheyne–Stokes respiration, or Kussmaul respiration patterns—dangerous patterns, indeed. The ability to bring various types of tools forward in the detection and identification of clinically significant patterns is just another way in which surveillance using PCD data is important to understanding the overall state of the patient.

The next chapter will consider clinical applications of PCD data, and these will assist in facilitating an understanding of how the methods just described can augment identifying patient adverse events.

Chapter 5

Clinical Workflows Supported by Patient Care Device Data

The focus of this chapter is on several clinical use cases that illustrate how data obtained from PCDs are used to facilitate clinical decision-making. As was discussed in Chapter 1, there are a number of high-value clinical conditions that can result in patient deterioration over time as reflected through vital signs measurements obtained from PCDs. Examples of these clinical conditions include systemic inflammatory response syndrome (SIRS), opioid-induced respiratory depression (OIRD), right ventricular (RV) and congestive heart failure (CHF), management of post-operative mechanical ventilation, and many others [12, 13, 84, 85]. A review of these individually now will serve to highlight how PCD data can be used to effect clinical surveillance.

5.1 Opioid-Induced Respiratory Depression (OIRD)

One example of respiratory deterioration that has been widely recognized in recent years is that of OIRD, in which patients recovering from surgeries and receiving postoperative pain medications may experience adverse reactions in the form of depressed respiratory states. Cases of sentinel events related to postoperative opioid-induced respiratory depression have been reported widely in the literature and the effects of postoperative respiratory depression have also been described by many clinicians and researchers [15, 20, 21, 67, 84, 86–89].

Table 5.1   The Top Five U.S. States Reporting Opioid-Related Inpatient Stays per 100,000 Population

Location	Rate of inpatient stay (×100,000)
Maryland	403.8
Massachusetts	393.7
District of Columbia	388.8
Rhode Island	377.4
New York	360.5

Source: Agency for Healthcare Research and Quality

The Agency for Healthcare Research and Quality (AHRQ) report on opioid-related inpatient hospital stays by state (as of 2014) indicated that Maryland, Massachusetts, the District of Columbia, Rhode Island, and New York are the top five locales in terms of inpatient stays. The rates per 100,000 population are shown in Table 5.1 [90, 91].

Claims that the opioid crisis in the United States has become "one of the worst health crises in US history" is backed by evidence that, in 2015, "more than 90 Americans died every day from opioid overdoses" [92].

The effects of prescribed opioids in the inpatient setting is further complicated by those patients who are addicted to or who are at-risk for adverse events related to pain medication AAMI has reported that "[o]pioids are involved in almost half of all deaths attributed to medication errors" [93].

A conference on opioid patient safety was convened in late 2014 in Chicago and research statistics reported described the scope of the patient safety challenge and urgent need for resolution, highlighting that "up to a third of all code blue arrests in hospitals" could be the result of OIRD [94].

Patients experiencing adverse events, including cardiac arrest, on the general care floor make up a significant portion of these reports. A study of 40 million hospitalized patients estimated that costs associated with postoperative respiratory failure total US$2 billion [95].

Further underscoring these findings is the issue of failure to detect potentially mortal respiratory failure in patients. One study estimated that on inpatient wards (i.e., general care floors), nursing staff did not detect 90% of patients who had one continuous hour of oxygen saturation below 90% (a measure of hypoxemia in adult patients) [86, 96].

Delays or inability to recognize early onset of respiratory events and the resulting respiratory depression, respiratory failure, and respiratory arrest suggest that continuous physiological monitoring inside of the hospital and even monitoring of patients receiving opioids for pain medication in ambulatory care settings (i.e., home) can have a measurable positive impact on patient adverse events and preventable mortality. Based on their research, Morris et al. reported that the incidence of inpatient, in-hospital respiratory failure was "associated with a mortality of nearly 40%" [15]. Moreover, the cause of death may not have been principally due to respiratory failure itself, but as a consequence of worsening respiratory function. Morris went on to describe categories of respiratory compromise, summarized below:

■ Impaired control of breathing, particularly in groups receiving sedation, those that have a central nervous system injury, those with neuromuscular diseases, and those using opioids.
■ Impaired airway protection, particularly in groups similar to those described in bullet 1, with the added cohort of groups suffering with laryngeal lesions and gastroesophageal regurgitation.
■ Increased airway resistance, either due to obstruction or constricted airways.
■ Parenchymal lung disease, particularly in groups diagnosed with preexisting disease, pneumonia, SIRS, and preexisting systemic co-morbidities.
■ Hydrostatic pulmonary edema, particularly in groups suffering from left-ventricular dysfunction, severe mitral or aortic valve pathology, and hypertensive crisis.
■ Right ventricular failure, particularly in groups with pulmonary embolism, pulmonary hypertension, and those suffering from chronic thromboembolic pulmonary hypertension (CTEPH).

From Wong et al., Based on reports made to the US Food and Drug Administration (FDA) between 2005 and 2009 [97]:

> more than 56,000 adverse events and 700 patient deaths were linked to patient-controlled analgesia (PCA) pumps. One out of 376 post-surgical patients are harmed or die from errors related to … [PCA] … that help relieve pain after surgical procedures.

Furthermore, Wong reported that slightly more than 70% of hospitals surveyed indicated they would prefer a "single indicator that accurately incorporates key vital signs, such as pulse rate (PR), peripheral oxygen saturation (SpO$_2$), respiratory rate (f_R) and end-tidal carbon dioxide (etCO$_2$)." Furthermore, "19 in 20 hospitals" indicated that they are concerned with alarm fatigue, and 90% would likely increase use of patient care devices if false alarms could be reduced.

As was discussed in Chapter 2, alarm reporting from PCDs is key to alerting clinical staff of adverse events. Yet, the alarm fatigue associated with responding to many nuisance alarms may result in clinical staff missing real events, or cause the machine alarms to be ignored or even turned off, negating any potential benefit of alarms at all.

Yet, data can tell a story. Time-series data, when taken into account with other contextual information surrounding a patient, can provide an indication of trends that would not be visible when viewed as discrete pieces of information, such as standalone alarm signals. Comparison among data elements over time provides not only the absolute value (e.g., the behavior of interval variables) but also the relationship with respect to the earlier time (e.g., behavior of ratio variables).

To illustrate, consider a sample of data as shown in Figure 5.1: a plot of patient end-tidal carbon dioxide (etCO$_2$) versus time. The end-tidal or expiratory carbon dioxide is a measure of the adequacy of ventilation and can be obtained through side-stream measurements via nasal cannula.

Normal values for etCO$_2$ span the range of 35–45 mmHg [125]. The data shown in this figure fall considerably outside of this range, as illustrated

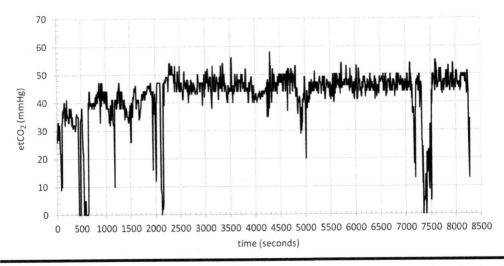

Figure 5.1   End-tidal carbon dioxide time-series versus time. Measurements obtained via capnography. (Data source: author.)

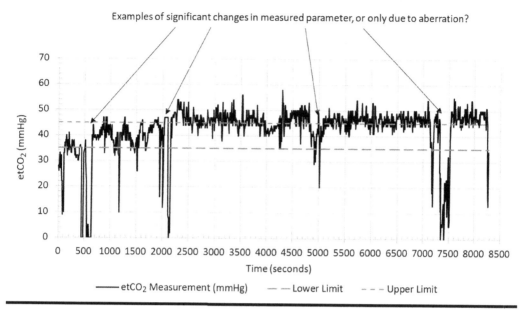

Figure 5.2 **Measured end-tidal carbon dioxide time-series highlighting locations in time of significant changes. (Data source: author.)**

in Figure 5.2. Conditions unique to the patient may indicate whether such deviations from established thresholds are acceptable and safe, and these are to be determined by the clinicians attending the patient.

Figure 5.2 illustrates where significant deviations outside of the threshold guardrails of 35–45 mmHg exist. What is the cause of this? Many possible answers exist, ranging from the artifact in the measurement associated with patient movement to true clinical events, such as sleep apnea. Note measurement variation can be spurious, or can trend or repeat cyclically, as was discussed in Chapter 4. Changes and events can be rapid and, possibly, significant as indicated by the arrows in Figure 5.2. When considering continuous monitoring of end-tidal CO_2, simple threshold alarms that annunciate when alarm signal deviations occur beyond threshold can, as is plainly visible in this figure, result in almost continuous alarm notifications that may prove to be entirely non-actionable.

Clinically actionable events may be more readily identified if other corroborating information can be included in making assessments, such as correlated or corresponding changes in respiratory rate, heart rate, and oxygen saturation values. Moreover, if clinically actionable events are truly present it would be logical to conclude that these events would either persist or would increase in frequency over time. That is to say, if there is a problem that requires intervention and is not self-correcting, then the problem will continue (e.g.: sleep apnea) or the problem will get worse (e.g.: complete cessation of breathing or cardiac arrest), which will most definitely require an intervention to correct.

The benefit of multi-parameter threshold alarms comes to mind here: changes in independently measured parameters that individually demonstrate clinically significant behavior bring authenticity to the concern that the changes in multiple parameters, when taken together, are genuinely related events that require intervention.

Thus, when comparing parameters such as peripheral oxygen saturation, respiration rate, and heart rate, one can obtain an understanding of these corroborated or (possibly) correlated behaviors. Consider the plots of Figure 5.2 through 5.5, which depict end-tidal carbon dioxide, peripheral oxygen saturation, respiration rate, and pulse rate, respectively. All of these parameters are plotted as time series measurements.

Peripheral oxygen saturation, or SpO_2, is plotted in Figure 5.3 against the same time window as the previous $etCO_2$ parameter of Figure 5.2. The limit threshold for this parameter, defined based on clinical guidelines and per organizational protocols and requirements, is defined at 90%, identified by the dashed line in Figure 5.3. Referring to the figure, note that in the range from approximately 1,800–2,000 seconds, the value of SpO_2 takes a downward plunge, rises back up again, and then later, at approximately 3,500 seconds, oscillates both below and above the threshold. Upon comparing

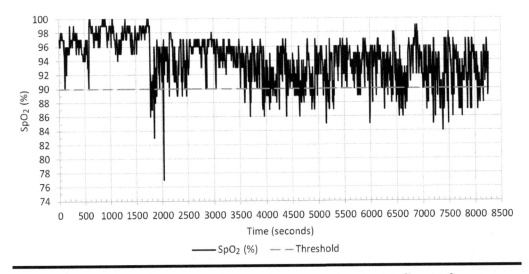

Figure 5.3 Peripheral oxygen saturation measurement corresponding to the same patient and time window as the previous end-tidal carbon dioxide measured parameter. The gray horizontal bar corresponds with an arbitrary threshold setting of 90%. (Data source: author.)

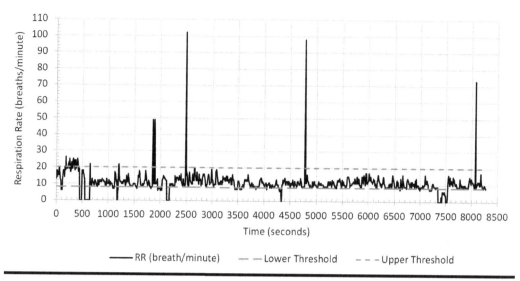

Figure 5.4 **Respiration rate versus time showing threshold limits of 8 and 20 breaths per minute (lower and upper limits, respectively). (Data source: author.)**

the noted event of Figure 5.3 with the same point in time within Figure 5.2, it is observed that there is a rapid reduction (or spike) downward in $etCO_2$ as well. Figure 5.4 illustrates the respiration rate, f, versus time. It can be seen by inspection that just after 2,000 seconds the respiration rate drops to zero. This coincides with a similar decline in $etCO_2$ at approximately the same time. In this instance, respiration rate and end-tidal carbon dioxide happen to be measured using the same nasal cannula, whereas peripheral pulse oximetry and heart rate are measured using a finger sensor. The decline in respiration and end-tidal carbon dioxide may have been due to the dislodging of the nasal cannula, or may have been due to apnea (i.e., cessation in breathing). The decline in the value of SpO_2 may have been due to dislodging of the pulse oximetry sensor or may have been due to the cessation in breathing, resulting in a decline in the blood oxygen saturation level.

Pulse rate shows some interesting behavior near the start of measurement, with measurements within the normal range, but then rising to the level of what may be in the range of sinus tachycardia, as shown in Figure 5.5. In viewing these plots individually, it can be rather difficult to discern correlations among parameters. A way to illustrate a concomitant association among parameters is by calculating the individual cross-correlations among the individual parameters and then plotting these cross-correlations over time.

Note that in computing correlation, the parameter that is computed is the correlation coefficient which ranges between -1 and 1. A correlation coefficient of -1 between two parameters indicates a relationship between the two

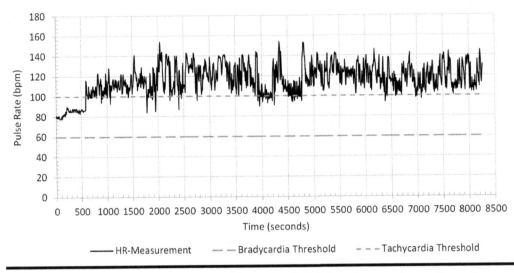

Figure 5.5 Pulse rate versus time showing thresholds for sinus tachycardia and bradycardia of 100 and 60 beats per minute, respectively. (Data source: author.)

in which as one parameter increases, the correlated parameter decreases in direct proportion to the first parameter. In contrast, a correlation coefficient of 1 indicates a direct relationship in which an increase in the first parameter results in a direct increase in the correlated parameter. These two instances are referred to as perfect inverse correlation (i.e., correlation coefficient of -1) and perfect direct correlation (i.e., correlation coefficient of 1), respectively. When the correlation coefficient is computed to be 0, this means no direct relationship or association between any two parameters.

As shown in Table 5.2, the computed cross-correlations (quantified by the *correlation coefficient* – see Equation 5.3) among the several parameters are calculated. In summary, the various cross-correlations represented in this table include:

- Respiratory rate versus:
  - End-tidal carbon dioxide
  - Pulse rate
  - SpO_2
- End-tidal carbon dioxide versus:
  - Pulse rate
  - SpO_2
- Pulse rate versus SpO_2

Notable in Table 5.2 are those instances in which the correlation coefficients between respiration rate and end-tidal carbon dioxide is either less than

Table 5.2 Correlations among etCO$_2$, SpO$_2$, PR, and RR Based on 30 Seconds of Running Time-Series Measurement Data

Time (seconds)	RR (breath/ minute)	etCO$_2$ (mmHg)	PR (beat/ minute)	SpO$_2$ (%)	30-second correlations					
					RR-etCO$_2$ correlation coefficient vs. time (seconds)	RR-PR correlation coefficient vs. time (seconds)	RR-SpO$_2$ correlation coefficient vs. time (seconds)	etCO$_2$-PR correlation coefficient vs. time (seconds)	etCO$_2$-SpO$_2$ correlation coefficient vs. time (seconds)	PR-SpO$_2$ correlation coefficient vs. time (seconds)
450	0	0	84	95	0.991	0.795	0.854	0.770	0.881	0.756
456	0	0	87	95	0.999	−0.120	0.913	−0.125	0.919	−0.066
462	0	0	86	95	1.000	−0.174	0.928	−0.174	0.928	−0.097
468	0	0	85	95	1.000	0.000	0.926	0.000	0.926	0.114
996	10	44	109	99	−1.000	0.639	−0.919	−0.639	0.919	−0.526
1014	12	39	111	98	−0.884	−0.249	−1.000	0.336	0.884	0.249
2058	14	47	136	92	0.919	0.597	0.928	0.769	0.946	0.841
2064	15	47	138	96	0.932	0.050	0.857	0.341	0.948	0.533
2940	14	46	131	97	0.886	−0.210	0.837	−0.632	0.944	−0.644
5526	10	46	123	91	−0.841	0.187	0.932	−0.127	−0.833	−0.078
7974	13	47	138	96	−0.962	−0.317	−0.961	0.134	0.912	0.264

−0.8 or greater than 0.8, corresponding to the cases in which a relatively high correlation (either positive or negative) is established between these two parameters. Interestingly, those instances in which high correlation coefficient is observed between respiration rate, end-tidal carbon dioxide, and oxygen saturation corresponds with those cases in which sleep apnea is detected (first four rows of the table) or where borderline hypercarbia is experienced (i.e., high end-tidal or expiratory carbon dioxide, typically associated with low respiration rate). This observation demonstrates how incorporating multiple parameters into a measure can serve to increase the likelihood of identifying a genuine adverse event as the likelihood that more than one parameter (or more than two parameters, in this case) will demonstrate a correlated behavior without some underlying cause is unlikely. Hence, an alarm signal that is transmitted to a clinician indicating such correlated behavior among parameters regarding carries a higher likelihood of more clinically actionable meaning over standalone threshold-based single parameter alarm signals.

The correlation coefficient provides a convenient measure of establishing possible association between or among parameters. One can also investigate the time-based interrelationships among parameters, such as whether one parameter expresses a behavior before another parameter indicates a change. This type of lead-lag interrelationship associated among parameters can also be reflected through *phase shift* between two parameters. The *lag* (i.e., *phase shift*) defines the amount of time by which behaviors in one signal may precede or follow those of another signal. For example, consider a sine and cosine wave, as illustrated in Figure 5.6, in which two signals are displayed:

$$S_1(t) = 10\sin\left(\pi \times \frac{t}{10}\right) \tag{5.1}$$

$$S_2(t) = 10\cos\left(\pi \times \frac{t}{10}\right) \tag{5.2}$$

The lower plot of Figure 5.6 represents the cross-correlation between the two signals represented in Equation 5.1 and 5.2, and reflects the relationship, the two signals have with respect to one another. The two signals correlate perfectly when they are shifted by an amount equal to 5 seconds in time, with signal 2 preceding or "leading" signal 1 by 5 seconds.

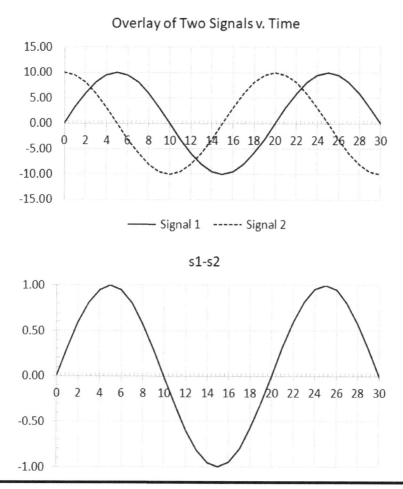

Figure 5.6 Example of two signals (sine and cosine, top figure) and the autocorrelation of the two signals (lower figure). Signal 1 and signal 2 are out of phase, with signal 2 "leading" signal 1 by 5 seconds.

Equation 5.3 defines the correlation coefficient between two signals:

$$\rho_{S1-S2} = \frac{Cov\left(S_1 S_2\right)}{\sqrt{Var\left(S_1\right) \times Var\left(S_2\right)}} \tag{5.3}$$

Where:
  $Cov(S_1 S_2)$ is the covariance between the two signals, and
  $Var(S_1)$ and $Var(S_2)$ are the signal variances respectively.

applied four time-series variables plotted in Figures 5.2 through 5.5, which illustrates the resulting cross-correlations among parameters plotted versus time across the span of all signal measurements.

The covariance is defined according to Equation 5.4:

$$Cov(S_1 S_2) = \frac{\sum_{i=1}^{N}(S_1(t) - \hat{S}_1)\sum_{j=1}^{N}(S_2(t) - \hat{S}_2)}{N-1} \qquad (5.4)$$

Where:

$$\hat{S}_1 = \frac{1}{N}\sum_{i=1}^{N} S_1(t) \qquad (5.5)$$

$$\hat{S}_2 = \frac{1}{N}\sum_{i=1}^{N} S_2(t) \qquad (5.6)$$

The variances are defined according to Equations 5.7 and 5.8, respectively:

$$Var(S_1) = \frac{\sum_{i=1}^{N}(S_1(t) - \hat{S}_1)^2}{N-1} \qquad (5.7)$$

$$Var(S_2) = \frac{\sum_{i=1}^{N}(S_2(t) - \hat{S}_2)^2}{N-1} \qquad (5.8)$$

The assumption is that the number (quantity) of data points for both samples are the same. Hence, N corresponds to the quantity of data points for each signal.

The plots of Figure 5.7 reflect the cross-correlation coefficients of the parameter measurements previously shown in Figures 5.2 through 5.5. The resulting calculation of cross-correlations over time in Figure 5.7 are displayed as follows. Beginning with the top left and moving clockwise:

■ Respiration rate—end-tidal carbon dioxide
■ Respiration rate—oxygen saturation
■ Pulse rate—oxygen saturation
■ End-tidal carbon dioxide—oxygen saturation

In all of these plots, there are slightly positive or negative cross-correlations. Yet, in the respiration rate—end-tidal carbon dioxide cross-correlation, a positive correlation that declines to near zero is noted, indicating that the change in end-tidal carbon dioxide generally precedes the change in respiration rate for the patient. In this way, clinical causality can be tested: the

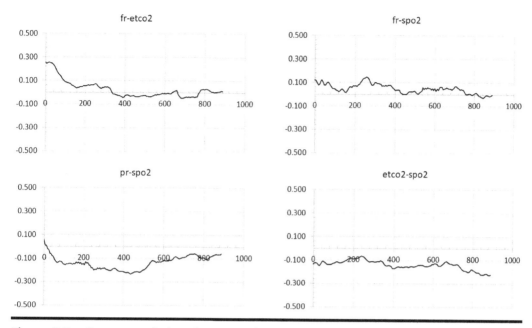

Figure 5.7 **Cross-correlations between the signal measurements of a patient under consideration.**

demonstrated mathematical interrelationships among parameters tend to validate the underlying physiological relationships, which provides evidence to support the claim that the mathematical relationships are probably not due to artifact or noise.

5.2 Patient Monitoring in Higher Acuity Settings

The physiological monitoring of patients occurs in most, if not all, locations within the healthcare enterprise. The fact that monitoring occurs is, perhaps, not a question. More importantly, in terms of physiological monitoring, a question: what type and how much surveillance is performed, required, and appropriate for patient safety considerations? Data are at the heart of clinical decision-making, and data from connected PCDs are unique in that they can be obtained regularly and objectively. Yet, measurements from PCDs can be subject to error inasmuch as some values may not be indicative of true physiological measurements when sensors obtain inaccurate readings, when calibration errors exist, when equipment malfunctions occur, or when sensors are intentionally moved or removed from a patient. Hence, all measurements require clinical validation to affirm their integrity. The cautionary aspects of data accuracy and integrity aside, PCD data can serve as a key tool in clinical decision support applications and functions. The focus here is on those hospital areas or units within which PCD data are used extensively for patient care management and treatment. These typically include intensive care units (ICUs), operating rooms (ORs), emergency departments (EDs), and ancillary units surrounding pre- and postsurgical care. Perhaps the highest acuity environments, such as ICUs and ORs, provide the best examples of the benefits brought to the clinical workspace associated with obtaining physiological monitoring data because it is in these environments that patients are most often dependent upon PCDs for life (i.e., patients are *technologically dependent*). Perhaps a good example of technological dependency is the patient who requires mechanical ventilation to sustain breathing function.

Many patients are mechanically ventilated in ICUs. That is, patients receive supplemental support to aid breathing via the use of an external mechanical ventilator that either assists or takes over the process of breathing for the patient entirely. Mechanically ventilated patients run the risk of higher incidents of hospital-acquired infections (HAIs), and, in particular, sepsis (or septicemia) and ventilator-acquired or ventilator-associated pneumonia (VAP) [98]:

> Ventilator associated pneumonia (VAP) … common in the intensive care unit (ICU), affecting 8 to 20% of ICU patients and up to 27% of mechanically ventilated patients … Mortality rates in patients with VAP range from 20 to 50% and may reach more than 70% when … infection is caused by multi-resistant and invasive pathogens.

HAIs and, in particular, septicemia, is the presence of bloodborne bacteria that (can) result in an inflammatory response most commonly known or referred to as sepsis. Although some may use the terms interchangeably, doing so is not accurate [99]. A blood infection has the potential to affect any patient, but particularly those with compromised immune systems, especially in ICUs. Sepsis can result in death if left untreated. The literature describes two classes of patients—the old and the very young—that are most susceptible to sepsis [100]:

> Sepsis is the 10th most common cause of death in the United States and its management has been estimated to cost 17 billion dollars

annually. Seventeen percent of all patients who develop sepsis have a malignancy as an underlying co-morbidity.

[A]s many as 10% of all cancer deaths (46,729 annual deaths) are attributable to sepsis.

Late-onset neonatal sepsis (LONS) is also of critical concern in newborns [101]:

Earlier detection and treatment of LONS offers the best opportunity to improve outcomes. … [Continuous] monitoring of neonatal heart rate characteristics … has been developed for earlier diagnosis and treatment of LONS in [neonatal intensive care unit (NICU)] patients.

The use of data obtained from continuously monitored vital signs has had encouraging results in terms of early detection of sepsis in ICU patients. Measurement of heart rate and respiratory rate variability has been linked to early sepsis onset [100]:

Heart rate and respiratory rate variability, when measured continuously, provide non-invasive metrics for detecting the early onset of sepsis … the presence of at least two of four clinical signs, including abnormalities in heart rate, temperature, respiratory rate and white blood cell count or its differential count, herald the onset of sepsis and … these conditions manifest many hours before the actual diagnosis.

Identifying deviations in normal vital signs has been recognized as useful in identifying deterioration and can herald the onset of adverse events even hours beforehand: [Abnormal] vital signs can help identify clinical deterioration in patients [between minutes and hours] before a serious adverse event occurs [102].

Responding to adverse patient events has given rise to a collaborative clinical team that is focused on preventing further deterioration in patients in whom emergent conditions such as sepsis have arisen. The concept of the Rapid Response Team (RRT) was introduced in hospitals throughout the United States and Europe as a means of intervening in patient decline and decompensation prior to the onset of a mortal adverse event for which there

Table 5.3   Rapid Response Team (RRT) Activation Characteristics: An Example

Characteristic	Code Team	Rapid Response Team
Activation criteria	No recordable pulse, blood pressure, respiratory effort, and generally unresponsive	Low blood pressure (hypotension); tachycardia (rapid pulse); respiratory distress (rapid breathing or tachypnea; slow breathing or bradypnea; difficulty breathing or dyspnea); altered level of consciousness
Typical assessments and treatments	Cardiac arrest; respiratory arrest; airway obstruction	Sepsis; pulmonary edema; arrhythmias; respiratory failure
Team composition	Anesthesia Fellow; ICU Fellow; Internal medicine house staff; ICU nurse	ICU Fellow; ICU nurse; Respiratory therapist; Internal medicine house staff
Call rate (per 1000 admissions)	0.5–5	20–40
In-hospital mortality rate (%)	70–90	0–20

is a risk associated with failure to rescue (FTR).* Key measures for the early onset warnings that trigger the deployment of such teams include changes in vital signs that may herald the onset of possibly irreversible cardiac, neurologic, or respiratory deterioration in patients, resulting in the potential for "failure to rescue" in the case of adverse events. In one multi-center study, the RRT was compared with the features and functions of the traditional Code Blue Team (CBT) with results showing a marked improvement in the number of in-hospital mortalities [102]. These results have been adapted into the format shown in Table 5.3.

In another study [103], characteristics associated with RRT activation were evaluated in a cohort of 474 patients, and the key reasons for activating were summarized as:

1) Hypotension (21.5%)
2) Respiratory distress (18.4%)
3) Altered level of consciousness (17.7%)

---

* Institute for Healthcare Improvement (IHI): "known by some as the Medical Emergency Team ... is a team of clinicians who bring critical care expertise to the bedside."

4) Tachycardia (11.2%)
5) Low oxygen saturation < 90% (9.9%)
6) Hypertension (4.2%)
7) Chest pain (3.4%)
8) Staff concern (2.7%)
9) Seizure (2.3%)
10) Other (bradycardia, tachypnea, arrhythmia, etc.) (8.7%)

The results of this study show the value of continuous vital signs monitoring to facilitate and herald the onset of conditions that, if left unchecked, can lead to the rapid deterioration of patients. While call rates are vastly increased over the traditional Code Blue Team activation, as shown in Table 5.3, it is noted that reductions in overall mortality rate are reported by almost an order of magnitude over the traditional Code Blue Team.

Examples of physiological parameters that can be readily measured in ICUs include heart rate or pulse, respiratory rate, temperature, and white blood cell count. Study findings also relate particular value thresholds that have been found consistent with the detection of sepsis onset and include [103]:

■ Heart rate > 90 beats per minute
■ Respiration rate > 20 breaths per minute or partial pressure of carbon dioxide in the bloodstream at or below 32 mmHg (i.e., $PaCO_2 < 32$ mmHg)*
■ Temperature > 38.0°C or < 36.0°C
■ White blood cell count (WBC) > 12,000 cells/mL, < 4000 cells/mL, or > 10% bands

These parameters are readily measured or obtained from PCDs and comprehensive metabolic panels. But, where in the hospital can one expect to find PCD data to support these types of calculations? PCD integration is most often employed within:

■ Cardiac-catheterization labs
■ Emergency departments
■ General care units
■ Intensive care units

---

* Note: by proxy, end-tidal carbon dioxide is a less invasive measure and can approximate the value of $PaCO_2$ obtained through arterial blood gas measurement.

- Medical/surgical units
- Operating rooms/surgery
- Other procedural areas (e.g., endoscopy, same-day surgery, ambulatory surgery)
- Postanesthesia care units
- Radiology (e.g., computed tomography, magnetic resonance imaging, X-ray, ultrasound)

Within these environments, PCD data are obtained on patients and is used for to assess the status of patients primarily through assessment of their cardiovascular and respiratory states: the bodily functions most associated with maintaining life. Data collection in these environments varies in quantity, type, and frequency. Table 5.4 provides examples of the frequencies of data collection and types of physiological measurements typically obtained in the specified hospital inpatient care unit. Note that the measurements obtained include both physiological data (to which the "Frequency of patient care device measurement" column refers), and other data that are typically collected in the particular hospital unit.

More departments exist than those shown in the table and more and different types of specialty measurements are obtained depending on the type of patient, condition, medical necessity, and so on. But, Table 5.4 describes the basic measurements usually obtained from patients within these principal locations. The information requirements from patients are based upon the needs of the physician and other care providers to effect treatment and patient care management. Patient care device measurements frequently "communicate" for the patients in the higher acuity care settings by relaying the cardiovascular and respiratory system performance as it responds to treatment. This is particularly true of the sedated patient who is unable to communicate verbally with the clinician. Patients may spend days or even weeks as inpatients. Hence, physiological monitoring may extend as long in these higher acuity settings.

Having provided a general overview and an initial treatment of monitoring in higher acuity settings, the following section focuses on the specifics of managing the mechanically ventilated patient to illustrate how data obtained from these therapeutic devices can be employed to facilitate clinical surveillance.

Table 5.4 Physiological Measurements and Data Collection Frequency Chart

Unit/ward	Function measured	Frequency of patient care device measurement	Duration
Emergency department	Heart (e.g., pulse, ST segments); comprehensive metabolic panel (i.e., laboratory measurements, including arterial blood gases; "Chem 14"*); perfusion (e.g., O_2 saturation); temperature	Continuous	Hours
Operating room/surgery	Heart (e.g., pulse, ST segments); perfusion (e.g., O_2 saturation, end-tidal CO_2); pulmonary (e.g., breath rate, tidal volume); temperature; drug administration	Continuous	Hours
Cardiac-catheterization laboratory	Heart (e.g., pulse, ST segments); perfusion (e.g., O_2 saturation)	Ad hoc	<< 1 day
Intensive care unit	Heart (e.g., pulse, ST segments, cardiac output, ejection fraction); perfusion (e.g., O_2 saturation, end-tidal CO_2); pulmonary (e.g., breath rate, tidal volume); temperature; comprehensive metabolic panel; intravenous and other drug administration; outputs	Continuous	Hours → days → weeks
Medical/surgical	Heart (e.g., pulse); comprehensive metabolic panel; perfusion (e.g., O_2 saturation); temperature	Ad hoc	Days-weeks
Radiology	Heart (e.g., pulse); perfusion (e.g., O_2 saturation)	Ad hoc	Hours

*Also known as a comprehensive metabolic panel. This is a collection of 14 tests that are used for monitoring specific health conditions and organ function. Tests include glucose, calcium, albumin, total protein, sodium, potassium, bicarbonate and carbon dioxide, chloride, blood urea nitrogen, creatinine, alkaline phosphatase, alanine amino transferase, aspartate amino transferase, and bilirubin.

Source: J. R. Zaleski, *Connected Medical Devices: Integrating Patient Care Data in Healthcare Systems*, Chicago, IL: HIMSS, 2015.

5.3 Mechanically Ventilated Patients

Many patients, particularly those in intensive care, will receive therapy in the form of mechanical ventilation. Some patients require mechanical ventilation postoperatively as a consequence of surgery (e.g., coronary artery bypass grafting or CABG). Others will require mechanical ventilation as a consequence of illness (e.g., chronic obstructive pulmonary disorder or COPD, COVID-19, etc.). Some patients in intensive care are either admitted in association with a postsurgical event or a preexisting ailment, while others will have been transferred due to a chronically worsening condition from another care unit within the hospital (e.g.: transfer from the general care floor post rapid response or code team activation). For instance, patients who have undergone coronary bypass grafting (CABG) surgery will require postoperative mechanical ventilation to support respiratory function while they are recovering from the effects of anesthesia and are monitored closely within the ICU. Mechanical ventilation, while a therapeutic function normally used in the ICU setting, is not restricted to use in that environment. Patients with acute ailments who are in a home care or in long-term acute care facilities may also receive mechanical ventilation. Such patients who receive mechanical ventilation therapy in these settings may be receiving ventilatory assistance via tracheostomy versus endotracheal tube (ETT) for post-operative mechanical ventilation.

Mechanical ventilation not only increases the complications and cost of treatment, but it also exposes patients to the likelihood of infection. Because the patients in this environment tend to be elderly and can have several co-morbidities, these patients are also prone to ailments that can exacerbate their reasons for being in the unit as well as their decline over time. Hospital acquired infections (HAIs) and ventilator associated pneumonia (VAP) can result in mortality and become real threats the longer the stay in intensive care is and the longer the duration of mechanical ventilation. One study on the duration and costs of patients in intensive care related to mechanical ventilation made the following finding [104]:

> … compared with patients who were not mechanically ventilated … [mean] intensive care unit cost and length of stay were $31,574 … [or] 14.4 days … for patients requiring mechanical ventilation and $12,931 … [or] 8.5 days for those not requiring mechanical ventilation.

As stated above, patients remaining in intensive care longer become targets for HAIs, and particularly VAPs. VAP is "pneumonia that occurs 48–72 hours or thereafter following endotracheal intubation." It is estimated to occur in anywhere from 9–27% of patients who are mechanically ventilated and the highest risk of contracting VAP is typically early in hospitalization. Mortality is highly variable and it has been estimated at between 33% and 50% in VAP [105].

HAIs impact both quality of life and the bottom line. One estimate, based on a population of 2,238 patients diagnosed with VAP, assessed the absolute cost between those having been diagnosed with VAP and those without at more than US$39,800 [106]. For these reasons, a considerable effort has been undertaken to reduce the onset, from improved knowledge awareness associated with compliance with clinical guidelines on hand washing, to algorithms that take information from multiple sources and process them to identify the early onset of HAIs [107].

For these reasons, a considerable effort has been undertaken to apply various to reducing the likelihood of onset, from compliance with clinical guidelines on handwashing to algorithms that can take information from multiple sources and process them to identify the early onset of HAIs [121].

Clinical surveillance and close monitoring provide the tools for early detection of events as well as assisting in determining whether interventions are required to prevent or decelerate worsening decompensation that can lead to failure to rescue. Methods that can identify worsening or advancing decompensation in patients can be among the several tools available to the clinician, which include order entry systems, electronic medical record systems, and clinical decision support systems [108]. The following section delves further into the details associated with managing one special class of mechanically ventilated patient.

5.4 Clinical Surveillance of the Mechanically Ventilated Patient

Patients can survive while being managed on mechanical ventilation for many years, and, with regular maintenance, can live out their lives with continuous mechanical ventilation. Other patients, particularly those recovering from surgery, will normally be removed or weaned from post-operative mechanical ventilation within several hours to several days postoperatively. In the latter case, removing the patient from mechanical ventilation is done gradually and on the basis of how well the patient can assume spontaneous respiratory function [38].

One technologically dependent class of patient is the patient who has undergone open heart coronary artery bypass grafting, or CABG surgery.

These patients, immediately postoperatively, are unable to sustain spontaneous respiration because of the various anesthetic, analgesic, and paralytic agents they receive during surgery which are still present within their systems postoperatively. Furthermore, in traditional open-heart surgery, the heart and lungs are usually stopped during the bypass grafting procedure. Hence, by procedure's end, patients are not normally breathing spontaneously and are completely dependent upon life-sustaining mechanical ventilation to maintain respiratory function.

Many CABG patients arrive from surgery with cardiovascular instabilities and co-morbidities in addition to complex acid-base disturbances which can affect the manner in which they metabolize oxygen and carbon dioxide. Patients who are able to be weaned rather directly from postoperative mechanical ventilation are normally those, as prescribed by clinical protocols and guidelines, who are free of these complicating factors. Furthermore, patients who are weaned from postoperative mechanical ventilation are those whose physiological and metabolic system parameters remain within normal ranges. Such patients are also free of acute neurological events (e.g.: coma or altered level of consciousness) and impaired autonomic nervous system activity that could otherwise disable spontaneous respiration [38].

The human respiratory system comprises two major sub-systems:

- a controlled physiological subsystem inclusive of the chest wall muscles, lungs, carbon dioxide, and oxygen stores; and,
- a controlling subsystem, inclusive of respiratory neurons and mechanical and chemoreceptors which transmit control commands to the controlled subsystem.

The purpose of the lungs is to extract oxygen and at the same expel carbon dioxide with each breath. During CABG surgery, the patient is administered a series of drugs that have the effect of depressing respiratory and cardiovascular function. Because of their effect, these drugs will cause the cessation of spontaneous breathing below life-sustaining levels. Two such indicators of life-sustaining lung function are respiration rate, f_R, and tidal volume, V_t (the volume of air inspired in a normal breath). Respiration rate is measured in terms of the number of breaths per minute. The tidal volume is a measure of the amount of air taken into the lungs during the course of a normal breath. In a resting state, the typical human breathes effortlessly at about 12 breaths per minute and a tidal volume commensurate with physiological characteristics associated with the size and weight of the individual and general health. A tidal volume of 5 mL/kg is typically used as a guideline for spontaneous respiratory function [38].

Sustaining spontaneous respiratory function when the respiratory system has been chemically depressed chemically requires the use of an external means of respiration to maintain the process of perfusion. Hence, the need for the mechanical ventilator.

After surgery, the CABG patient is brought from the OR into the ICU. Once the patient has arrived, he or she is transferred to a mechanical ventilator. Adult patients are typically initiated at a level of mandatory breathing on the mechanical ventilator of between 10 and 12 breaths per minute. Each mandatory breath initiated by the ventilator causes a specific volume of mixed air to enter the lungs. The preset mandatory tidal volume is assigned by respiratory therapy at a level typically based on protocols of 5 mL/kg of ideal body weight. Normally, a small amount of positive pressure is maintained within the lungs in order to increase perfusion. This pressure, commonly referred to as positive end-expiratory pressure (PEEP) is set at the beginning of ventilation. A value of 5 cmH_2O is common in patients not experiencing any pulmonary or cardiovascular problems [38] [109, pp. 468–481].

Oxygen is administered initially through the mechanical ventilator at a level exceeding that of room air (i.e., 21%). This is usually referred to as the fraction of inspired oxygen (FiO_2), and is then reduced to room air once the patient's blood oxygenation level is determined and verified as being within a normal range. By the time of endotracheal tube extubation inspired oxygen fraction is normally around 21% (room air).

Because the cardiovascular and respiratory systems of the patient are depressed during this postoperative stage, they require help in providing the body and all of its sub systems with oxygenated blood. One way to ensure that enough oxygen is received by the body is to ventilate the patient on high levels of pure oxygen. As the patient's cardiovascular and respiratory systems regain their natural function, the amount of oxygen is reduced. Pulse oximetry is used and calibrated against arterial blood-gas (ABG) oxygenation measurements several times to verify the accuracy of these non-invasive pulse oximetry measurements.

Prior to endotracheal tube extubation, each patient must satisfy specific criteria relative to blood-gas oxygen and carbon dioxide levels, which are measures of whether the patient is breathing and oxygenating adequately. Patient respiratory parameters such as respiratory rate, inspiratory force, and vital capacity must also satisfy certain thresholds prior to discontinuation of mechanical ventilation and endotracheal tube extubation.

Weaning from mechanical ventilation can proceed once the patient awakens and initiates spontaneous breathing. The mandatory respiratory rate setting of the ventilator is reduced by the respiratory therapist on the orders of the attending physician in time intervals ranging from minutes to hours. The rate at which mechanical support is decreased is determined based on observing the patient's spontaneous respiratory rate and the state of the patient's physiology and metabolic system response. General practice guidelines call for maintaining the total patient respiratory rate within a range prescribed per practice guidelines (e.g.: between 8 and 20 breaths per minute). Over the span of several hours, the patient will be weaned to spontaneous breathing mode, in which the patient has assumed full mechanical responsibility for breathing while still attached to the mechanical ventilator. A determination will be made as to whether the patient is able to support spontaneous breathing without the aid of mandatory ventilatory support. This determination is accomplished by observing and measuring several parameters related to spontaneous ventilatory effort, including the consciousness of the patient, the arterial oxygen saturation and carbon dioxide levels, and the frequency and depth of spontaneous breathing.

Once the patient begins breathing spontaneously, the attending physician may assess the patient's ability to breathe without the aid of the mechanical ventilator by initiating spontaneous breathing trials. This process is highly empirical from the decision perspective as some patients who meet the criteria for extubation may exhibit the ability to sustain spontaneous breathing, but end up not being able to continue breathing without assistance, whereas others may be able to meet the criteria and be successfully weaned from postoperative mechanical ventilation.

A patient's ability to sustain spontaneous breathing is determined by the level of carbon dioxide in the bloodstream, and the patient's stamina based on the ability to support the volume and pressure loads placed on the patient's respiratory muscles. These volume and pressure loads are assessed using specific tests (i.e., the negative inspiratory force and vital capacity tests). The volume loads are evaluated by measuring the minute ventilation requirements of the patient, typically in terms of "dead space" volume versus tidal volume, or V_D/V_T. The term "dead space" refers to air that is inhaled during breathing but that does not take place in the gas exchange process. The relationship between dead space ventilation and tidal volume is given by Equation 5.9 [110]:

$$\frac{V_D}{V_T} = \frac{PaCO_2 - PeCO_2}{PaCO_2} \tag{5.9}$$

Where:

$PaCO_2$ is the partial pressure of carbon dioxide in the bloodstream; and,
$PeCO_2$ is the mixed expired partial pressure of carbon dioxide.

The pressure loads are typically expressed with respect to the volume delivered over time. The integral of the pressure over the volume delivered is oftentimes referred to as the Work of Breathing (WoB), which is the integral of pressure and volume, and is given by Equation 5.10 [111, p. 203]:

$$WoB = \int pdV = \int p\dot{V}_E dt \tag{5.10}$$

Where:

$\dot{V}_E$ is the time rate of expired volume change;
P is pressure; and,
dt is the infinitesimal variable over which the integration takes place.

A normal work of breathing for a healthy adult is in the range of approximately 0.35 joules/liter [112].

Objective measures of the tolerance for weaning through spontaneous breathing trials vary based on protocol and patient. In general, adequate oxygenation, breathing effort, and normal blood chemistry are sought as the most basic signs of respiratory adequacy [1, 2, 38].

$$\frac{f_R}{V_T} < 105 \tag{5.11}$$

One measure that has been used as a simple determinant of the successful ability to wean from mechanical ventilation is the rapid-shallow breathing index (RSBI) developed originally by Yang and Tobin [113]. The RSBI ratio of respiratory rate to tidal volume is defined in Equation 5.11. The ratio of respiration rate to tidal volume during spontaneous breathing trials as a scalar assessment of likelihood that a patient could be successfully extubated. Yang and Tobin had determined in their original research findings that a patient who experienced a ratio below 105 during the period of spontaneous breathing trials was less likely to be successfully extubated than a candi-date with a ratio value above 105.

The process by which patients are liberated from postoperative mechanical ventilation can vary by institution and has evolved over the years. Many new modes of ventilatory support available in modern mechanical ventilators have brought new techniques to bear on the process of regaining spontaneous breathing. But, the diagram of Figure 5.8 provides a general flow of the usual steps involved in the process of regaining spontaneous respiratory function in the recovering CABG patient [1, 2, 38].

The diagram of Figure 5.8 is decomposed into three major phases, described by the two light-shaded areas and a middle dark-shaded area. The sloped or ramped interfaces between the phases are intended to identify that the transitions are not hard or fixed; that there is a graduated space in which weaning and attempts at evolving the patient to the next phase occurs, and these vary by patient.

The first or initial of these phases represents that in which patient breathing is supported almost entirely by the mechanical ventilator. This phase represents the case in which the patient has just arrived from surgery. For CABG patients undergoing open-heart surgery, they can arrive at the ICU fully sedated and fully dependent upon mechanical ventilation to support their respiratory function. The patient is typically cold (a consequence of the surgical environment). and sometimes arrive with core body temperatures well below normothermia (37°C). The patient must re-warm to ensure all internal organs are operating optimally.

In the second phase, which overlaps with the first, patients have ventilatory support reduced until they begin to breathe on their own. The rate of reduction and the modes of mechanical ventilation considered depend upon the patient response, the clinical judgment of the physician, and the protocols normally employed by the care team for ventilatory support reduction. The support reduction is accomplished in combination with multiple sources of information, including results from comprehensive metabolic panels and arterial blood gas measurements, vital signs, imaging, and bedside assessment.

Once the patient is breathing spontaneously, vital signs obtained from cardiovascular and respiratory measurements as well as those obtained from metabolic panels are monitored to ensure that the patient is not decompensating. The weaning process also involves the adjustments (i.e., reduction, removal, administration) of intravenous drugs. An example of one key drug administered intravenously during this process is sodium nitroprusside—a vasodilator. This is normally used to reduce afterload on the already-prone heart, which may require many hours to recover normal function postoperatively.

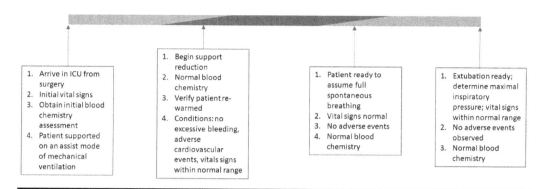

Figure 5.8 An example of an algorithm for postoperative weaning from mechanical ventilation.

In the third phase, the patient is usually breathing spontaneously. The patient is fully re-warmed and the mechanical ventilator is providing oxygen and pressure support in this phase. The patient's blood chemistry will be re-evaluated through further metabolic panels, and any evidence of adverse events will be assessed (e.g.: chest-tube drainage, rapid breathing, circulatory and neurological issues, etc.). The patient will be evaluated to determine the viability for endotracheal tube extubation. Prior to extubation, a chest X-ray may be ordered to verify that the lungs are clear.

Given all conditions are greenlighted and protocols are satisfied, a breathing trial process can commence and involves measurement of the maximal negative inspiratory pressure (or force), NIF, in which the conscious patient is asked to inhale against a closed valve circuit (that is, disconnected from the ventilator) or, while still attached to the ventilator, the machine will be used to measure the maximal negative inspiratory force and vital capacity, V_c. Maximal negative inspiratory pressures in excess of a specified threshold (e.g.:≥ 24cmH$_2$O; protocol dependent) and adequate vital capacities (e.g.: ≥ 1 liter) are used as indicators of a patient's viability to support adequate spontaneous respiration and, together with good blood gas data, are indicators for extubation.

The list below defines typical vital signs and metabolic measurements that are used as part of overall clinical surveillance [1, 2, 38, 109]:

1) Pulse rate or heart rate (PR or HR) in units of beats per minute;
2) Arterial systolic, diastolic, and mean blood pressures (ABP_S, ABP_D, ABP_M) in units of mmHg;
3) Arterial oxygen saturation SaO$_2$ obtained from metabolic panel or from pulse oximetry (SpO$_2$) in units of %;

4) Drug administrations (e.g.: Nitroglycerin and sodium nitroprusside dosage levels);

5) Cardiac output (CO), measured or calculated as the product of heart rate and stroke volume. Non-invasive cardiac output monitoring may be in place as well;

6) Venous oxygen saturation (SvO_2) if monitors are available, in units of %;

7) Patient core temperature (T_c) in units of Celsius;

8) Central venous pressure (CVP) in units of mmHg;

9) Pulse pressure (mmHg), the difference between systolic and diastolic pressure;

10) Partial pressure of carbon dioxide ($PaCO_2$) in arterial blood, in units of mmHg;

11) Partial pressure of oxygen (PaO_2) in arterial blood, in units of mmHg;

12) Base excess (BE) in units of mEq/L. Note that BE is an indicator of acid-base disorders and can be approximated using Equation 5.12 [114]:

$$BE = 0.9287 \times \left[HCO_3^- - 24.4 + 14.83 \times \left(pH - 7.4 \right) \right] \tag{5.12}$$

13) Bicarbonate concentration (HCO_3^-) in units of mEq/L;

14) Sodium concentration (Na^+) in units of mEq/L;

15) Potassium concentration (K^+) in units of mEq/L;

16) Calcium concentration (Ca^+) in units of mg/dL or mmol/L;

17) Blood acidity-alkalinity (pH);

18) Hemoglobin level in units of grams per deciliter;

19) Urine output in units of milliliters per day or milliliters per hour;

20) Blood loss in units of cubic centimeters per hour;

21) Intravenous drug administrations;

22) Mandatory respiratory rate and spontaneous respiratory rate (f_R^m and f_R^s) in units of breaths per minute;

23) Mandatory tidal volume and spontaneous tidal volume (V_T^m, V_T^s) in units of liters per breath;

24) Mandatory minute volume and spontaneous minute volume (V_M^m, V_M^s) in units of liters per minute;

25) Dynamic compliance—change in lung volume per unit change in pressure in the presence of flow—in units of milliliters per cm H_2O [115];

26) Static compliance—change in lung volume per unit change in pressure in the absence of flow—in units of milliliters per cm H_2O [115];

27) Inspired O_2 fraction (FiO_2) in units of %;

28) Other ventilatory parameters relating to pressure, settings, gas mixing, etc.; and,

29) Non-numeric parameters (e.g., consciousness, skin coloration).

Technologically dependent patients such as those heart patients being weaned from postoperative mechanical ventilation can experience adverse events for which clinical surveillance is necessary to ensure their continuing successful recovery. Certain complications must be monitored as these adverse events could lead to death or permanent injury, and can preclude the weaning process from continuing [1, 2, 38, 109]:

1) Excessive bleeding from chest tubes (in excess of ~100 cubic centimeters per hour);

2) Poor left-ventricular heart function, including low cardiac output, arrhythmias, S-T segment elevations, etc.;

3) Abnormal brain function;

4) Poor oxygen saturation or lung injury; and,

5) A physician's decision to preclude a patient from weaning and/or extubation based on a combination of these or any other problems.

From the perspective of clinical surveillance, accepted definitions of weaning success and failure vary and have evolved over the years. Published protocols have specified criteria for weaning success and failure. One example has been sustained spontaneous breathing for 72 hours without mechanical assistance required post extubation of the endotracheal tube. Similarly, respiratory "failure" has been defined as [116]:

1) Inability to maintain arterial carbon dioxide pressure $PaCO_2$ and pH within acceptable limits, as determined by blood-gas measurements.

2) Inability to maintain PaO_2 at an acceptable level, as determined from arterial blood-gas measurements and SpO_2.

3) Patient exhaustion resulting from the attempt to maintain adequate PaO_2, $PaCO_2$, and pH levels, caused by hyperventilation and respiratory rates in excess of approximately 24 breaths per minute.

In practical applications, patient care management surrounding weaning is complex. Yet the data collected from PCDs can assist clinical surveillance by providing the necessary moment to moment input on the status of the patient through cardiovascular and respiratory parameter measurements. Key sources of PCD data at the point of care in support of postoperative weaning from mechanical ventilation include:

1. **Mechanical ventilator**: provides inspiratory and expiratory parameters, rates, pressures, expiratory and inspiratory gas measurements, and work of breathing over time.
2. **Infusion pump**: used throughout the hospital and extensively in intensive care units in particular for intravenous drug administration, fluid administration, and therapies. Intensive care units are clinical settings in which a single patient may be receiving infusions from many drugs simultaneously (perhaps half-a-dozen or more), requiring many of infusion pumps.
3. **Physiological monitor**: supports continuous vital signs monitoring. Typical examples of continuously monitored parameters include heart rhythm, respirations, plethysmography, capnography, and blood pressure. These are essential adjuncts to maintain close watch in support of patient care management.
4. **Specialty devices**: equipment including non-invasive cardiac output monitors, intra-aortic balloon pumps, venous oxygen saturation, pulse oximeters, and temperature sensors are either available in standalone form factors or are available as adjuncts to existing physiological monitors and some mechanical ventilators.
5. **Comprehensive metabolic panels**: necessary for blood chemistry assessment and are essential for evaluating patient organ function and whether patients are experiencing acidosis or alkalosis together with determining arterial oxygen content and carbon dioxide content of arterial blood. Arterial blood gas assessments are essential in determining whether the body is metabolizing oxygen properly and the gas exchange process is proceeding normally.

Given a patient is being weaned from mechanical ventilation over time, then, as the mandatory component of respiratory rate is reduced, the total respiratory rate and tidal volume are monitored to determine whether the patient is breathing adequately in terms of respiration frequency and depth, and, therefore, the patient can begin breathing on his or her own.

All parameters taken together provide a view of the patient's state over time. The ability to determine the likelihood and safety to discontinue mechanical ventilation and extubate the patient is another example in which multi-parameter PCD data is essential. Viability to extubate must be determined via comparison with established weaning criteria. If a patient is compliant with the specified parameter thresholds and ranges, then the likelihood that the patient is following a beneficial path to extubation is higher than if the patient deviates from these pre-established ranges and settings. Thus, the combination of measurements obtained from the various PCDs provides the needed information for close surveillance of the patient's cardiac and respiratory systems, and deviations from these pre-established baselines are the triggers to initiate notification to clinical staff as to variances that may require intervention.

5.5 Systemic Infection and Shock

Patients who are at risk for systemic shock require close surveillance, as well. The human body is a complex system of sub-systems in which the inter-relationships among these sub-systems is key to understanding the overall "trajectory" or state of the patient's health. This trajectory is not established through consideration of single parameters, but by the totality of the patient assessment. The state of any patient is determined through a holistic and contextual evaluation that considers both subjective and objective measures, inclusive of observations, past medical history, history of present illness, vital signs, imaging, and the performance of multiple system functions. Systemic shock is an example of an imbalance experienced among these various sub-systems, and its onset is quite serious and can be fatal, if left unattended. Shock is related to the inability of the cardiorespiratory system to effectively *perfuse*. That is, failure to perfuse refers to the inadequate delivery of oxygenated blood to the cells and the inadequate removal of waste and carbon dioxide from the cells so as to offload these to the appropriate receiving systems, specifically, the lungs and kidneys.

Shock can be caused by many things, but it is subdivided into four distinct groups: [117, 118]

1. Hypovolemic shock: shock resulting from low blood volume as a result of blood loss or due to fluid loss (dehydration). The net result is hypoperfusion.
2. Distributive shock: shock resulting from loss of blood vessel (i.e., smooth muscle) tone, causing hypoperfusion to result. Example causes can be anaphylaxis. Bacterial or viral infections can cause the body to respond by dilating blood vessels to facilitate white blood cell transport.

The effect is hypoperfusion. Because of the systemic nature of the infection, however, the dilation becomes body wide. When blood vessels dilate, blood pressure goes down. Yet, the brain responds to the need for homeostasis and the heart rate increases in order to maintain cardiac output. This is why the shock index can be a good indicator of sepsis onset, as hypoperfusion is a chief indicator.

3. Cardiogenic shock: shock induced when the heart fails in its ability to circulate blood adequately. This can occur as a result of myocardial infarction, causing injury to the heart muscle, or in cases of physical trauma. Hypoperfusion also results.

4. Obstructive shock: blood is physically prevented from flowing. An example is pulmonary embolism. Blood is prevented from reaching essential organs, like portions of the lung, which results in hypoxia and necrosis.

In all of these cases, the result of the insult to the body is immediately measured through vital signs. The body rapidly changes or adjusts in attempts to compensate for the hypoperfusion. The brain signals the body's sympathetic nervous system ("fight-or-flight" response). This means heart rate increases and respirations increase. In compensated shock, patients will exhibit mental status changes, heart rate increases, respiration rate increases, delayed capillary refill, and pale and diaphoretic (sweaty, clammy) skin [117].

When the body cannot keep up with the insult and fatigue then it evolves from compensated shock to decompensated shock. In this case, less oxygen is delivered to the cells so that the diffusion in the cell transitions from the normal aerobic process of adenosine triphosphate (ATP) production to its anaerobic counterpart. How does this happen? Well, if the patient can no longer maintain respirations at the necessary rate, or if the heart weakens, for instance, and results in reduced circulation or circulation that is inadequate to sustain life, then perfusion declines and the body moves into decompensated shock. In this case, the cells produce energy from glucose anaerobically as well as lactic acid, and the patient becomes acidotic. While compensated shock requires the body's muscles to work harder, the body becomes fatigued, leading to an increased production of anaerobic waste products. Thus, compensatory mechanisms fail and decompensated shock results. Decompensated shock is characterized by severe hypoperfusion, decreased mental status, and, if no intervention is performed, this becomes irreversible and death follows.

Throughout this entire process, vital signs become a key indicator of normal or declining patient state. Moreover, vital signs, taken in concert with one another, provide an indicator of decompensation. For example, if the body is reacting to systemic infection (possibly caused by a urinary tract infection or other causes), and the patient develops a systemic infection resulting in hypoperfusion, the heart attempts to maintain circulation resulting from the vasodilation (i.e., expanding of the arterioles to allow for easier circulation) that mimics the behavior of the body's immune response. In an immune response, the arterioles widen to facilitate the movement of white blood cells through the circulatory system, which, in turn, seek out and destroy foreign microbes. Immediate measures that result from vasodilation include increased heart rate (pulse) as well as increased respirations to maintain oxygenation necessary for perfusion [118, pp. 670–4].

Patients who experience cardiorespiratory deterioration or shock are usually preceded by some type of physiological instability [118]. Yet, changes in vital signs that herald the onset of physiological instability may be more visible when taken together in combination with one another. A straightforward example of combining two parameters to yield a more informative combination is the Shock Index (SI). In one single-center study (Berger), it was determined that the Shock Index may be a simple indicator to assess the likelihood of clinical deterioration [116]. The Shock Index is defined in Equation 5.14 as a scalar parameter relating pulse and systolic blood pressure [119]:

$$SI = \frac{HR}{BP_{sys}} \tag{5.14}$$

Systolic blood pressure, BP_{sys}, referenced in Equation 5.14 may be obtained through a non-invasive blood pressure cuff measurement. Pulse or heart rate can also be obtained through normal bedside measurements such as pulse oximetry monitoring. In both of these instances, the physiological variables represent standard patient care device parameters that can be communicated directly from the bedside to end-point electronic medical record systems or other types of clinical information systems. Studies have also shown that sudden onset cardiac arrest and unexpected (unplanned) transfers from lower acuity in-hospital settings to the intensive care unit have been preceded by instabilities reflected through physiologic measurements [120].

Yet, often vital signs that are within a normal range, when taken together, are representative of conditions that merit further review. For instance, heart rate may be within a normal range, albeit at the uppermost end of the normal range (e.g., 100 beats per minute sinus rhythm). Yet, when taken together with another normal range parameter value, it may indicate a problem or may herald the onset of a problem, such as the case when blood pressure is marginally low (e.g., systolic blood pressure equal to 100 mmHg). Simple measures of performance can oftentimes be the most useful. The Shock Index falls into this category because it is a single parameter and requires very little interpretation. In the aforementioned study by Berger et al., patients having "...an abnormal SI of 0.7 or greater (15.8%) were three times more likely to present with hyperlactatemia than those with a normal SI (4.9%). The negative predictive value (NPV) of a SI $\geq$ 0.7 was 95%, identical to the NPV of SIRS". Furthermore, it was observed that "SI $\geq$ 0.7 performed as well as SIRS in NPV and was the most sensitive screening test for hyperlactatemia and 28-day mortality. SI $\geq$ 1.0 was the most specific predictor of both outcomes."

Hence, while a simple metric, shock index demonstrates the value of two relatively straightforward and simple measures: heart rate and blood pressure.

5.6 Intracranial Pressure Influences on Blood Pressure

Just as shock can influence blood pressure, changes in blood pressure can herald potentially dangerous events such as stroke and intracranial bleeding due to head trauma. When a patient experiences a stroke, also known as a cerebrovascular accident (CVA), two possible types of effects may occur:

1. Ischemic stroke: occurs when a blood clot blocks a cerebral blood vessel. It is estimated that 80% of CVAs are ischemic strokes [121].
2. Hemorrhagic stroke: occurs when a cerebral blood vessel ruptures, resulting in bleeding within the subdural cavity.

Changes or alterations in levels of alertness and responsiveness are typical in the case of stroke. But, in addition, and particularly in the case of hemorrhagic strokes, increases in blood pressure can and do result in increased intracranial pressure (ICP). As the pressure within the braincase (skull) increases due to bleeding within the skull, the brain can be forced down into the *foramen magnum* at the base of the skull (the entry point of the spinal cord). This not only causes changes in the patient level of consciousness, but the increasing pressure also results in changes in vital signs, including heart rate, respiration rate, and blood pressure. The increasing pressure at the base of the brain, where the medulla oblongata and the pons are centered, results in effects and changes in vital signs, in addition to the fact that the increasing pressure inside of the skull results in the need to counter that increasing pressure by raising the blood pressure in the arteries. This causes the heart to beat more forcefully and with greater volume, which causes the blood pressure in the body to rise concomitantly to counteract the increasing pressure within the skull. Needless to say, these are all emergent events and if not addressed directly, death can and often does result.

In the intensive care unit, influences on intracranial pressure include headboard angle and head trauma with subsequent brain swelling. Clinical surveillance is necessary in the case of CVA and head trauma as these patients require close monitoring for changes in intracranial pressure, blood pressure, and neurologic assessments.

The headboard (a.k.a. head-of-bed) angle can have an influence on ICP, as well. Studies have shown a relationship between ICP and the headboard angle [122]. The significance of this relationship can be very important in terms of governing the outcome for the patient. In particular, chief among these relationships is the cerebral blood flow (CBF) and cerebral perfusion pressure (CPP). The relationship between these two parameters is given by the Hagen–Poiseuille relationship, Equation 5.15 [109, 113, 123–125]:

$$CBF = \frac{CPP \cdot \pi \cdot R^4}{8\eta L} \qquad (5.15)$$

Where:

R is the arteriole radius;

η is the blood viscosity; and.

L is the vessel length.

The cerebral perfusion pressure is dependent on the pressure gradient between arteries and veins and is approximated by Equation 5.16:

$$CPP = MAP - ICP \qquad (5.16)$$

Where:

MAP is the mean arterial pressure and ICP approximates the mean cerebral venous pressure.

ICP can be readily measured by intraventricular catheters or subcutaneous sensors in the skull. Normal CPP ranges from 60–100 mmHg. Mean arterial pressure is approximated in accord with Equation 5.17:

$$\text{MAP} = \frac{2}{3}\text{BP}_{\text{DIAS}} + \frac{1}{3}\text{BP}_{\text{SYS}} \tag{5.17}$$

Where:

BP_{SYS} and BP_{DLAS} are systolic and diastolic blood pressure, respectively.

ICP values normally range under 10 mmHg, whereas precipitous drops in CPP can result in brain ischemia. Increases in CPP are typically due to increases in MAP. CBF has been observed to remain fairly flat over a wide range of MAP due to factors related to cerebral metabolism and *autoregulation*. A principal component of CBF in terms of influence is vessel radius, R. Increase in vessel radius is known as *vasodilation*. Vasodilation leads to increased cerebral blood flow and increased ICP. In turn, vasoconstriction (i.e., narrowing of arterioles) and dilation (i.e., widening of arterioles) are influenced by carbon dioxide, $PaCO_2$, concentrations. Metabolic measurements of $PaCO_2$ are regularly performed. Approximations for $PaCO_2$ are also measured through the exhalation circuitry of mechanically ventilated patients, referred to as end-tidal carbon dioxide or $etCO_2$, a parameter introduced earlier. Note that when gas exchange in the lungs is normal, then the difference between arterial and $etCO_2$ values is typically less than 5 mmHg [109].

A relationship exists between PaCO2 and CBF specifically in the $PaCO_2$ range from 30 through 80 mmHg [120]. Reductions in $PaCO_2$ result in vasoconstriction in cerebral vessels, reducing CBF and ICP. Yet, excessive reductions in $PaCO_2$ can result in brain ischemia. Nominal ranges of $PaCO_2$ of 35–45 mmHg, per weaning protocols, are designed to balance the competing effects leading to increases in ICP and ischemia. A factor that can impact CBF is blood viscosity primarily related to *hematocrit*. Hematocrit is measured and reported through comprehensive metabolic panels. Reduction in core body temperature also improves CBF tolerance [122]. Anesthetics and certain IV drugs can affect CBF through vasodilation, as well [38].

5.7 Chapter Summary

The focus of this chapter has been on taking a deeper dive into several clinical scenarios with the hopes of revealing some of the complexities and information needs of the clinician, with further implications on data collection and surveillance.

Vital signs can reveal "lurking" physiological behaviors, such as increasing heart rate and decreasing blood pressure, which can herald the onset of shock, or suddenly cause an increase in blood pressure post a cerebrovascular accident. Continuous monitoring of these patients is key to filling gaps that can identify patients who are undergoing both rapid and slow decompensation over time. A timely response to patient events as identified through changing physiological state can help to mitigate or avoid rapid responses, failures to rescue, and tragedies. When one can identify sentinel monitoring parameters then changes in these parameters provide clues into prospectively assessing a patient's possible decompensation. For example, if it is observed that a particular room location has an inordinately high quantity of machine-generated alarms related to heart rate, blood pressure, and respiration rate, then investigating whether the cause clinical or technical may be in order. Yet, excessive alarm signals generated on one patient may be due to the fact that the patient is agitated or perhaps due to poor or erratic measurements. These, too, are clinically relevant events that require intervention by a trained care provider in order to mitigate their occurrence. The key point is that the sources of aberrant measurements may be clinically actionable; may be actionable but not relevant to patient safety; or may be technical in nature or unrelated to a clinically actionable event. Hence, mitigation is necessary. A possible mechanism, therefore, is to consider which measurements, when they evolve in concert with one another, paint a more clinically meaningful picture as to the root cause in the patient. This is the essential message the author hopes to transmit to the willing reader.

Epilogue: Lessons Learned from Continuous Monitoring

Accurate measurements are essential for diagnosis and treatment. Data tell a story and guide assessments and understanding of patient acuity. Their accuracy is paramount. Throughout this text the message that has been repeated through examples is that continuous monitoring and tracking of multiple findings is necessary to support clinical surveillance. The various findings necessary to support continuous monitoring include physiological monitoring data obtained from patient care devices and other discrete information that complements this, such as results of comprehensive metabolic panels, observations, and imaging. The ensemble of these separate but interrelated pieces of information provides the overall view, or paints the picture, of the patient state: the trajectory and current representation of the patient right now that can be projected or propagated ahead in time to a future state.

For a patient who is deteriorating or at risk for deterioration with suspected cardiac or respiratory issues, understanding their multi-organ system health is a key indicator as to whether the patient will survive and what type of intervention or treatment must be administered in order to increase the patient's chances of survival. Oftentimes, multi-organ health may be visible through the patient's vital signs, physical appearance, and the patient's mental status.

Patient deterioration or improvement over time must also include that most important data element: time. This means the clinician needs to know whether a patient is improving or deteriorating over time, and how rapidly either is occurring. Thus, all measurements need to be accompanied by the time at which they are taken. Furthermore, measurements need to be obtained regularly to establish a trend in patient state. Sometimes a vital sign that is hastily taken can misguide a clinician. Measurements must always be validated to ensure they are accurate. Just because blood pressure or a pulse is taken using a physiological monitoring system does not mean the values obtained are correct. Oftentimes, training and experience can help validate whether, say, a blood pressure measurement or a pulse oximetry reading are within normal ranges or valid merely by observing the patient. If an automated blood pressure measurement is questionable or cannot be obtained reliably, auscultate using a manual cuff.

What are some of the lessons learned and examples as to where vital signs provide a key indicator of patient decompensation?

1. If a patient's systolic and diastolic blood pressures are growing closer together over time, then this decreasing pulse pressure can be a sign of cardiac tamponade and impending decompensation.

2. If a patient's blood pressure is increasing but his or her pulse is decreasing and breathing is becoming irregular (i.e. Cushing's triad), this can be a sign of increasing intracranial pressure.

3. A patient may be responsive or not; may have an injury or not; may have a medical condition or not. Yet, if nothing is visible on the outside of your patient, this does not mean that something serious may not be going on internally, and without imagery, it can be nearly impossible to tell what is happening with the patient. What medications is the patient receiving? Is there a possibility that the medications (or non-compliance relative to taking medications) can explain the vital signs state of the patient? A proxy for internal decompensation can be reflected through vital signs and observations of the patient's physical appearance.

4. Patient care device measurements are often required before administering certain medications. For example, if the patient's blood pressure is bordering on the low side (i.e., hypotensive), this can be a contraindication for vasodilators. Make certain that the patient can safely receive the medication and that it won't put the patient in a dangerously hypotensive state. Knowing whether the patient is on the borderline or is trending toward hypertension or hypotension over time is an essential bit of information in management and treatment.

5. If vital signs change, are they changing in a positive way, are they remaining stable, or are they changing in a negative way? Over what time span are vitals changing, and, if a critical patient, are these intervals frequent enough to catch rapidly changing events? Are events changing more rapidly now that an indication has been identified that a

patient is declining or improving at an increased rate? What is the implication of these changes?

6. Metabolic information also needs to be trended and incorporated into the findings. For example, trending the changes in creatinine or blood urea nitrogen and impacts on fluid retention and pulmonary edema, relating to shortness of breath and declining oxygen saturation. Understand the whole patient in terms of clinical decision-making from how they look and how they behave (e.g.: sluggishness, sleeping more often, unable to move as quickly, requiring assistance).

7. Significant changes in patient state are often reflected through multiple findings simultaneously. With the trend toward solving complex problems using machine learning, it is important to recognize that not every problem requires a complex solution. Simple trending or understanding the implications biologically, chemically, and medically of the interrelationships among parameters can lead to a clearer understanding of what is actually taking place within a patient and help to guide treatment through heuristics and expectations based on clinical training.

8. Take advantage of these heuristic relationships and make use of them to assist in guiding care. For example, systemic infection leads to vasodilation and leaking capillaries as white blood cells increase to attack the sources of the systemic infection. Patients can become hypotensive leading to distributive and hypovolemic shock. So, recognizing a decrease in systolic blood pressure trends over time is a warning that, systemically, a patient is decompensating. This can be recognized through continuous monitoring.

9. Do not assume that a single measurement taken every few hours paints an accurate picture of the patient. If your patient is truly stable, then this may be sufficient. But, if there is a possibility that instability can occur in your patient, or if you suspect an intervention can lead to or is recognized as possibly leading a patient toward unstable behavior, then it is necessary to continuously monitor the patient. What might be considered an intervention that would result in a patient possibly becoming unstable? The administration of pain medication could be one such example: patients tolerate opioids in different ways and effects that an opioid can have on respiratory systems and the brain can and have led to apnea and hypoxemia. Never make assumptions.

10. Do not ignore what the patient tells you about his or her past history and the history of the present illness. Do not ignore what the family

tells you about these, either. Remember: they need to live with this—the care provider does not. The patient and family are the greatest sources of subjective and valuable information regarding the condition the patient is experiencing, albeit oftentimes not wrapped around clinical training or clinical jargon. Seek this information as an important adjunct and heuristic to guide intervention and therapy, comfort, and pain management.

Technology needs to coexist within a high-touch environment. There is no substitute for looking at, listening to, and touching (palpating) the patient. Technology cannot replace this (at least not yet). Hence, looking at numbers from physiological monitoring systems and patient care devices without context is only gathering a portion of the story surrounding the patient. Clinical value is measured in terms of treating patients and in reducing the likelihood of adverse events. By analogy, just as a reduction in workflow steps implies reduced cost, a reduction in the likelihood of adverse events does the same.

Introducing new processes into operational healthcare environments presents challenges for many reasons, from regulatory and legal to practical operational concerns such as training and education of clinical, information technology, and biomedical staff members. The challenges related to obtaining data over the course of the past several years is giving way to the more clinically meaningful challenge of what to do with the data to improve patient safety, reduce noise, and improve the environment for both care provider and patient. While the mission is still rather daunting, it is the hope that in a small way this text helps to shed some light on the subject of clinical surveillance and the benefits that can be achieved using patient care device data to improve patient safety in the inpatient environment.

Bibliography

1. J. R. Zaleski, *Connected Medical Devices: Integrating Patient Care Data in Healthcare Systems*, Chicago, IL: HIMSS, 2015.
2. J. R. Zaleski, *Integrating Device Data into the Electronic Medical Record: A Developer's Guide to Design and a Practitioner's Guide to Application*, Erlangen: Publicis KommunikationsAgentur GmbH, GWA, 2009.
3. The Office of the National Coordinator for Health Information Technology, "Get the Facts About Electronic Health Records: Advancing America's Health Care," [Online]. Available: https://www.healthit.gov/sites/default/files/factsheets/ehrs-advancing-americas-health-care.pdf.
4. CDC, "Public Health and Promoting Interoperability Programs (Formerly, Known as Electronic Health Records Meaningful Use)," [Online]. Available: https://www.cdc.gov/ehrmeaningfuluse/introduction.html.
5. US Government, "Part III: Department of Health and Human Services: 45 CFR Part 170 – Health Information Technology: Initial Set of Standards, Implementation Specification, and Certification Criteria for Electroinic Health Record Technology; Final Rule," Federal Register, Washington, DC, Wednesday, 28 July 2010.
6. HIMSS Medical Device & Patient Safety Task Force, "Medical Device Meaningful Use Matrix: Impact of Medical Device Systems on Meaningful Use Strategy," [Online]. Available: https://www.himss.org/library/quality-patient-safety/medical-devices/meaningful-use.
7. J. R. Zaleski, *Medical Device Data and Modeling for Clinical Decision Making*, Norwood, MA: Artech House, 2011.
8. J. R. Zaleski, "Big Data for Predictive Analytics in High Acuity Health Settings," in *Big Data for the Greater Good*, Gewerbestrasse, Switzerland: Springer, 2019, pp. 51–100.
9. "clinical." Merriam-Webster.com. *Merriam-Webster*, 2019. Web. 10 December 2019.
10. "surveillance." Merriam-Webster.com. *Merriam-Webster*, 2019. Web. 10 December 2019.
11. B. Saugel, P. Hoppe and A. K. Khanna, "Automated Continuous Noninvasive Ward Monitoring: Validation of Measurement Systems Is the Real Challenge," *Anesthesiology*, 2020.

12. ECRI - Patient Safety, "2019 Top 10 Patient Safety Concerns: Executive Brief," 2019. [Online]. Available: https://www.ecri.org/landing-top-10-patient-safety-concerns-2019.

13. ECRI - Technology, "2019 Top 10 Health Technology Hazards: Executive Brief," October 2019. [Online]. Available: https://www.ecri.org/Resources/Whitepapers_and_reports/Haz_19.pdf.

14. NASA, [Online]. Available: https://www.nasa.gov/sites/default/files/images/269792main_GPN-2000-001210_full.jpg.

15. T. A. Morris, P. C. Gay, N. R. MacIntyre, D. R. Hess, S. K. Hanneman, J. P. Lamberti, D. E. Doherty, L. Chang and M. A. Seckel, "Respiratory Compromise Is a New Paradigm for the Care of Vulnerable Hospitalized Patients," *Respiratory Care*, vol. 62, no. 4, pp. 497–512, 2017.

16. J. P. Curry and C. R. Jungquist, "A Critical Assessment of Monitoring Practices, Patient Deterioration, and Alarm Fatigue on Inpatient Wards: A Review," *Patient Safety in Surgery*, vol. 8, no. 29, 2014.

17. L. A. Lee, R. A. Caplan, L. S. Posner, G. W. Terman, T. Voepel-Lewis and K. B. Domino, "Postoperative Opioid-Induced Respiratory Depression," *Anesthesiology*, vol. 122, pp. 659–65, 2015.

18. S. Greenberg, "Opioid-Induced Ventilatory Impairment: An Ongoing APSF Initiative," *APSF Newsletter*, vol. 32, no. 3, February 2018.

19. R. K. Gupta and D. A. Edwards, "Monitoring for Opioid-Induced Respiratory Depression," *APSF Newsletter*, vol. 32, p. 3, February 2018.

20. A. K. Khanna, D. I. Sessler, Z. Sun, A. J. Naylor, J. You, B. D. Hesler, A. Kurz, P. J. Devereaux and L. Saager, "Using the STOP-BANG Questionnaire to Predict Hypoxaemia in Patients Recovering from Noncardiac Surgery: A Prospective Cohort Analysis," *BJA*, vol. 116, no. 5, pp. 632–40, 2016.

21. C. R. Jungquist, D. J. Correll, L. A. Fleisher, J. Gross, R. Gupta, C. Pasero, R. Stoelting and R. Polomano, "Avoiding Adverse Events Secondary to Opioid-Induced Respiratory Depression: Implications for Nurse Executives and Patient Safety," *JONA*, vol. 46, no. 2, pp. 87–94, 2016.

22. S. M. Lauritsen, M. Kristensen, M. V. Olsen, M. S. Larsen, K. M. Lauritsen, M. J. Jorgensen, J. Lange and B. Thiesson, "Explainable Artificial Intelligence Model to Product Acute Critical Illness from Electronic Medical Records," 3 December 2019. [Online]. Available: https://arxiv.org/abs/1912.01266.

23. A. A. Kramer, "A Novel Method Using Vital Signs Information for Assistance in Making as Discharge Decision from the Intensive Care Unit: Identification of Those Patients at Highest Risk of Mortality on the Floor or Discharge to a Hospice.," *Medical Research Archives*, vol. 5, no. 12, 2017.

24. J. R. Moorman, W. A. Carlo, J. Kattwinkel, R. L. Schelonka, P. J. Porcelli, C. T. Navarette, E. Bancalari, J. L. Aschner, M. W. Walker, J. A. Perez, C. Palmer, G. J. Stukenborg and D. E. Lake, "Mortality Reduction by Heart Rate Characteristic Monitoring in Very Low Birth Weight Neonates: A Randomized Trial," *The Journal of Pediatrics*, vol. 159(6), pp. 900–906, 9 August 2011.

25. D. E. Lake and J. R. Moorman, "Accurate Estimation of Entropy in Very Short Physiological Time Series: The Problem of Atrial Fibrillation Detection in Implanted Ventricular Devices," *American Journal of Physiology - Heart and Circulatory Physiology*, vol. 300, pp. H319–325, 29 October 2010.

26. M. Bailey, "Hospital Alarms Prove a Noisy Misery for Patients: 'I Feel Like I'm in Jail.'," *The Washington Post*, 12 December 2019.

27. M. M. Pelter and B. J. Drew, "Harm from Alarm Fatigue," November 2015. [Online]. Available: https://psnet.ahrq.gov/web-mm/harm-alarm-fatigue.

28. M. Cvach, "Monitor Alarm Fatigue: An Integrative Review," *Biomedical Instrumentation & Technology*, vol. 46(4) pp. 268–277, 2012.

29. AAMI, "Clinical Alarm Management Compendium," Association for the Advancement of Medical Instrumentation (AAMI), Arlington, VA, 2015.

30. M. Cvach, *Managing Monitor Alarms: Lessons Learned*, Baltimore, MD: The Johns Hopkins Hospital, 2011.

31. AAMI, "Clinical Alarms 2011 Summit Convened by AAMI, FDA, TJC, ACCE, and ECRI Institute," AAMI, Arlington, VA, 2011.

32. J. Spetz, N. Donaldson, C. Aydin and D. S. Brown, "How Many Nurses per Patient? Measurements of Nurse Staffing in Health Services Research," *Health Serv Res*, vol. 43, no. 5 Pt 1, pp. 1674–1692, October 2008.

33. S. A. Glasmacher and W. Stones, "Anion Gap as a Prognostic Tool for Risk Stratification in Critically Ill Patients -- A Systematic Review and Meta-Analysis," *BMC Anesthesiology*, vol. 16, no. 68, 2016.

34. M. Cattabiani, "$6 Million Recovery: Girl Dies Following Tonsillectomy" 21 April 2014. [Online]. Available: https://www.rossfellercasey.com/news/6-million-recovery-girl-who-died-following-routine-tonsillectomy/.

35. "Promise to Amanda Foundation," [Online]. Available: http://promisetoamanda.org. [Accessed August 2019].

36. "Physician-Patient Alliance for Health & Safety," [Online]. Available: http://www.ppahs.org. [Accessed August 2019].

37. J. R. Zaleski, *Modeling Post-Operative Respiratory State in Coronary Artery Bypass Grafting Patients: A Methodology for Weaning Patients from Post-Operative Mechanical Ventilation*, Philadelphia, PA: University of Pennsylvania, 1996.

38. Integrating the Healthcare Enterprise, "Integrating the Healthcare Enterprise Patient Care Device Domain," [Online]. Available: https://www.ihe.net/ihe_domains/patient_care_devices/.

39. CapSite, *2012 Medical Device. Integration Study*, Capsite, 2015.

40. Black Box SME, *Quantifying the Business Value of Medical Device Connectivity*, Mesa, AZ: Black Box SME, 2011.

41. The Association for the Advancement of Medical Instrumentation (AAMI), "AAMI White Paper 2012: Medical Device Interoperability: A SaferPath Forward. Priority Issues from the AAMI-FDA Interoperability Summit," AAMIFDA, 2012.

42. WestHealth Institute, "The Value of Medical Device Interoperability," March 2013. [Online]. Available: https://www.westhealth.org/wp-content/uploads/2015/02/The-Value-of-Medical-Device-Interoperability.pdf.

43. Healthcare Innovation, "Hospitals Looking at EHR Integration," 24 June 2013. [Online]. Available: https://www.hcinnovationgroup.com/interoperability-hie/infrastructure/news/13019998/report-hospitals-looking-at-ehr-integration. [Accessed August 2019].

44. J. M. Rodrigues, A. Kumar and C. Bousquet, "Using the CEN/ISO Standard for Categorical Structure to Harmonise the Development of WHO International Terminologies," in *Medical Informativcs in a United and Healthy Europe*, Amsterdam, the Netherlands: IOS Press, 2009, p. 255.

45. I. A. Mitchell, H. McKay, C. Van Leuvan, R. Berry, C. McCutcheon, B. Avard, N. Slater, T. Neeman and P. Lamberth, "A Prospective Controlled Trial of the Effect of a Multi-Faceted Intervention on Early Recognition and Intervention in Deteriorating Hospital Patients," *Resuscitation*, vol. 81, no. 6, pp. 658–666, 2010.

46. J. Whittington, R. White, K. Haig and M. Slock, "Using an Automated Risk Assessment Report to Identify Patients at Risk for Clinical Deterioration," *The Joint Commission Journal on Quality and Patient Safety*, vol. 33, no. 9, pp. 569–574, 2007.

47. Evidence-Based Synthesis Program (ESP) Center | Portland VA Medical Center | Portland, OR, "Early Warning System Scores: A Systematic Review," Department of Veterans Affairs | Health Services Research & Development Service, Portland, OR, 2014.

48. AAMI, FDA, TJC, ACCE, ECRI, "A Siren Call to Action: Priority Issues from the Medical Device Alarms Summit," Association for the Advancement of Medical Instrumentation, Arlington, VA, 2011.

49. A. C. Bridi, T. Q. Louro and R. C. Lyra da Silva, "Clinical Alarms in Intensive Care: Implications of Alarm Fatigue for the Safety of Patients," Revista Latino-Americana de Enfermagem, vol. 22, no. 6, pp. 1034–40, 2014.

50. I. MacDonald, "Hospitals Rank Alarm Fatigue as Top Patient Safety Concern," *Fierce Healthcare*, 22 January 2014.

51. M. C. Chambrin, P. Ravaux, D. Calvelo-Aros, A. Jaborska, C. Chopin and B. Boniface, "Multicentric Study of Monitoring Alarm in the Adult Intensive Care Unit (ICU): A Descriptive Analysis," *Intensive Care Medicine*, vol. 25, pp. 1360–1366, 1999.

52. F. Schmid, M. S. Goepfert and D. A. Reuter, "Patient Monitoring Alarms in the ICU and in the Operating Room," *Critical Care*, vol. 17, no. 216, 2013.

53. K. J. Ruskin and J. P. Bliss, "Alarm Fatigue and Patient Safety," *APSF Newsletter*, vol. 34, no. 1, June 2019.

54. American Association of Critical-Care Nurses, "AJCC Article: Most Alarms Are Not Clinically Relevant," 9 January 2018. [Online]. Available: https://www.aacn.org/newsroom/ajcc-article-most-alarms-are-not-clinically-relevant?sc_camp=CD43C0BB8FD44F21938E9979D8EA2220. [Accessed 17 February 2020].

55. H. Ruppel, M. Funk and R. Whittemore, "Measurement of Physiological Monitor Alarm Accuracy and Clinical Relevance in Intensive Care Units," *American Journal of Critical Care*, vol. 27, no. 1, pp. 11–21, 2018.

56. B. J. Drew, P. Harris, J. K. Zegre-Hemsey, T. Mammone, D. Schindler, R. Salas-Boni, Y. Bai, A. Tinoco, Q. Ding and X. Hu, "Insights into the Problem of Alarm Fatigue with Physiolopgic Monitor Devices: A Comprehensive Observational Study of Consecutive Intensive Care Unit Patients," *PLOS ONE,* vol. 9, no. 10, 2014.

57. K. Lansdowne, D. G. Strauss and C. G. Scully, "Retrospective Analysis of Pulse Oximeter Alarm Settings in an Intensive Care Unit Patient Population," *BMC Nursing,* vol. 15, no. 36, 2016.

58. J. Welch, B. Kanter, B. Skora, S. McCombie, I. Henry, D. McCombie, R. Kennedy and B. Soller, "Multi-Parameter Vital Sign Database to Assist in Alarm Optimization for General Care Units," *Journal of Clinical Monitoring and Computing,* vol. 30, pp. 895–900, 2016.

59. P. Cosper, M. Zellinger, A. Enebo, S. Jacques, L. Razzano and M. N. Flack, "Improving Clinical Alarm Management: Guidance and Strategies," *BI&T,* vol. March/April, pp. 109–115, 2017.

60. S. D. Hall, "Joint Commission Outlines Dangers of Alarm Fatigue," 9 April 2013. [Online]. Available: https://www.fiercehealthcare.com/it/joint-commissi on-outlines-dangers-alarm-fatigue. [Accessed 17 February 2020].

61. The Joint Commission, "Sound the Alarm: Managing Physiologic Monitoring Systems," *The Joint Commission Perspectives on Patient Safety,* vol. 11, no. 12, pp. 6–11, 2011.

62. CBS News, "Too Many Beeping Alarms to Blame for Dozens of Hospital Deaths per Year, Report Says," 8 April 2013. [Online]. Available: https://www .cbsnews.com/news/too-many-beeping-alarms-to-blame-for-dozens-of-hospital-deaths-per-year-report-says/. [Accessed 17 February 2020].

63. J. Devore and R. Peck. *Statistics: The Exploration and Analysis of Data* 5th ed., Thompson & Brooks/Cole, pp. 406–412, 2004.

64. K. Terry, "Improved Continuous Monitoring of Hospital Patients Boosts Staff Efficiency," *CIO,* 24 May 2017.

65. M. Vockley, "Healthcare System Takes Bold Step with Continuous Mointoring," *BI&T,* vol. July/August, pp. 312–317, 2017.

66. C. R. Jungquist, K. Smith, K. L. Wiltse Nicely and R. C. Polomano, "Monitoring Hospitalized Adult Patients for Opioid-Induced Sedation and Respiratory Depression," *AJN,* vol. 117, no. 3, pp. S27–S35, 2017.

67. M. Albur, F. Hamilton and A. P. MacGowan, "Early Warning Score: A Dynamic Marker of Severity and Prognosis in Patients with Gram-Negative Bacteraemia and Sepsis," *Annals of Clinical Microbiology and Antimicrobials,* vol. 15, no. 23, 2016.

68. Y.-c. Liu, J.-h. Liu, Z. A. Fang, G.-l. Shan, J. Xu, Z.-w. Qi, H.-d. Zhu, Z. Wang and X.-z. Yu, "Modified Shock Index and Mortality Rate of Emergency Patients," *World Journal of Emergency Medicine,* vol. 3, no. 2, pp. 114–117, 2012.

69. L. Kleeman, "Understanding and Applying Kalman Filtering," in *Proceedings of the Second Workshop on Perceptive Systems,* Perth, WA, 25–26 January 1996.

70. R. F. Souto, J. Y. Ishihara and G. A. Borges, "A Robust Extended Kalman Filter for Discrete-Time Systems with Uncertain Dynamics, Measurements and Correlated Noise," in *2009 American Control Conference / Hyatt Regency Waterfront*, St. Louis, MO, 10–12 June 2009.

71. R. Sameni, M. B. Shamsollahi and C. Jutten, "Filtering Electrocardiogram Signals Using the Extended Kalman Filter," in *Proceedings of the 2005 IEEE Engineering in Medicine and Biology 27th Annual Conference*, Shanghai, China, 1–4 September 2005.

72. L. Kleeman, *Understanding and Applying Kalman Filtering*, Clayton, VIC: Monash University, 2007.

73. G. Welch and G. Bishop, "An Introduction to the Kalman Filter - TR 95–041," Department fo Computer Science; University of North Carolina at Chapel Hill, Chapel Hill, NC, 27599–3175, 24 July 2006.

74. M. Saeed, M. Villarroel, A. T. Reisner, G. Clifford, L. Lehman, G. B. Moody, T. Heldt, T. H. Kyaw, B. E. Moody and R. G. Mark, "Multiparameter Intelligent Monitoring in Intensive Care II (MMIC-II): A Public-Access ICU Database," *Critical Care Medicine*, vol. 39, no. 5, pp. 952–960, May 2011.

75. A. L. Goldberger, L. A. Amaral, L. Glass, J. M. Hausdorff, P. C. Ivanov, R. G. Mark, J. E. Mietus, G. B. Moody, C. K. Peng and H. E. Stanley, "PhysioBank, PhysioToolkit, and PhysioNet: Components of a New Research Resource for Complex Physiologic Signals," *Circulation*, vol. 101, no. 23, pp. E215–E220, 13 June 2000.

76. T. Ruf, "The Lomb-Scargle Periodogram in Biological Rhythm Research: Analysis of Incomplete and Unequally Spaced Time-Series," *Biological Rhythm Research*, vol. 30, no. 2, pp. 178–201, 1999.

77. J. Púčik, "Heart Rate Variability Spectrum: Physiologic Aliasing and Nonstationarity Considerations," in *Trends in Biomedical Engineering*, Bratislavia, 16–18 September 2009.

78. C. S. Burrus, R. A. Gopinath and H. Guo, *Introduction to Wavelets and Wavelet Transforms--A Primer*, Prentice-Hall, 1998, p. 3.

79. T. Vuorenmaa, *The Discrete Wavelet Transform with Financial Time Series Applications*, 2003.

80. J. F. Zolman, *Biosatistics: Experimental Design and Statistical Inference*, Oxford University Press, 1993, pp. 77–99.

81. C. Torrence and G. P. Compo, "A Practical Guide to Wavelet Analysis," *Bulletin of the American Meteorological Society*, vol. 79, no. 1, pp. 69–71, January 1998.

82. S. Ross, *A First Course in Probability*, 3d Edition, Macmillan Publishing Company, 1988, pp. 336–357.

83. ECRI Institute, "Executive Brief - Top 10 Health Technology Hazards for 2017," ECRI Institute, Plymouth Meeting, PA, 19462–1298, November 2016.

84. AAMI Foundation Health Technology Safety Institute (HTSI), "Safety Innovations: Using Data to Drive Alarm Systems Improvement Efforts--The Johns Hopkins Hospital Experience," AAMI HTSI, 2012.

85. D. I. Sessler, *Where's the Evidence - What Exists, What Works, and What More Do We Need to Do?*, Boston, MA: ASA, 2017.

86. A. H. Taenzer and G. T. Blike, "Postoperative Monitoring--The Dartmouth Experience," *APSF Newsletter*, vol. 27, no. 1, Spring-Summer 2012.

87. D. Supe, L. Baron, T. Decker, K. Parker, J. Venella, S. Williams, K. Beaton and J. Zaleski, "Continuous Surveillance of Sleep Apnea Patients in a Medical-Surgical Unit," *BI&T*, pp. 236–51, May/June 2017.

88. B. Friedman, D. Fuckert, M. Jahrsdoerfer, R. Magness, E. S. Patterson, R. Ryed and J. Zaleski, "Identifying and Monitoring Respiratory Compromise: Report from the Rules and Algorithms Working Group," *BI&T*, pp. 110–22, March/April 2019.

89. A. J. Weiss, A. Elixhauser, M. L. Barrett, C. A. Steiner, M. K. Bailey and L. O'Malley, "Opioid-Related Inpatient Stays and Emergency Department Visits by State, 2009–2014; Statistical Brief #219," AHRQ Healthcare Cost and Utilization Project, Washington, DC, 2017.

90. J. R. Zaleski and R. Peruvemba, "The Analytic Link Between Population Health and Leading Hospital and Ambulatory Patient Safety Considerations," in *Analytics, Operations, and Strategic Decision Making in the Public Sector*, Hershey, PA: IGI Global, 2019, pp. 111–136.

91. IBM Research, "Combating the Opioid Epidemic with Machine Learning," IBM, 2017.

92. Assocation for the Advancement of Medical Instrumentation (AAMI), "Opioid Safety & Patient Monitoring Conference Compendium," Chicago, 2014.

93. J. P. Curry, "Postoperative Monitoring for Clinical Deterioration," in *Patient Safety in Surgery*, London: Springer-Verlag, 2014, p. 92.

94. K. Reed and R. May, "Healthgrades Patient Safety in American Hospital Study (p. 5)," March 2011. [Online]. Available: https://www.cpmhealthgrades.com/CPM/assets/File/HealthGradesPatientSafetyInAmericanHospitalsStudy2011.pdf.

95. T. Weingarten, *Respiratory Depression in Ambulatory Surgery Patients: Lessons from Inpatients*, Boston, MA: ASA, 2017.

96. M. Wong, A. Mabuyi and B. Gonzalez, "First National Survey of Patient-Controlled Analgesia Practices," A Promise to Amanda Foundation & The Physician-Patient Alliance for Health and Safety, March–April 2013.

97. A. Rea-Neto, N. C. Youssef, F. Tuche, et al., "Diagnosis of Ventilator-Associated Pneumonia: A Systematic Review of the Literature," *Critical Care*, vol. 12, p. R56, 2008.

98. T. Torrey and M. Menna, "Difference Between Sepsis and Septicemia," 10 January 2020. [Online]. Available: https://www.verywellhealth.com/sepsis-and-septicemia-2615130. [Accessed 2 March 2020].

99. A. R. Mato, B. D. Fuchs, D. F. Heitjan et al., "Utility of the Systemic Inflammatory Response Syndrome (SIRS) Criteria in Predicting the Onset of Septic Shock in Hospitalized Patients with Hematologic Malignancies," *Cancer Biology and Therapy*, vol. 8, no. 12, pp. 1095–1100, 2009.

100. K. D. Fairchild and M. T. O'Shea, "Heart Rate Characteristics: Physiomarkers for Detection of Late-Onset Neonatal Sepsis," *Clinics in Perinatology*, vol. 37, no. 3, pp. 581–598, 2010.

101. D. A. Jones, M. A. DeVita and R. Bellomo, "Rapid-Response Teams," *The New England Journal of Medicine*, vol. 365, no. 2, pp. 139–146, 14 July 2011.

102. J. M. Walston, D. Cabrera, S. D. Bellew, M. N. Olive, C. M. Lohse and M. F. Bellolio, "Vital Signs Predict Rapid-Response Team Activation Within Twelve Hours of Emergency Department Admission," *Western Journal of Emergency Medicine*, vol. XVII, no. 3, pp. 324–330, May 2016.

103. J. F. Dasta, T. P. McLaughlin, S. H. Mody and C. T. Piech, "Daily Cost of an Intensive Care Unit Day: The Contribution of Mechanical Ventilation," *Critical Care Medicine*, vol. 33, no. 6, pp. 1266–1271, June 2005.

104. A. A. Kalanuria, W. Zai and M. Mirski, "Ventilator-Associated Pneumonia in the ICU," *Critical Care*, vol. 18, no. 208, 2014.

105. M. H. Kollef, C. W. Hamilton and F. R. Ernst, "Economic Impact of Ventilator-Associated Pneumonia in a Large Matched Cohort," *Infection Control & Hospital Epidemiology*, vol. 33, no. 3, pp. 250–256, March 2012.

106. P. J. Pronovost, K. M. Sutcliffe, L. Basu and M. Dixon-Woods, "Changing the Narratives for Patient Safety", *Bull. World Health Organization*, vol. 95, pp. 478–480, 25 April 2017.

107. N. Adhikari and W. Sibbald, "The Large Cost of Critical Care: Realities and Challenges," *Anesthesia & Analgesia*, vol. 96, no. 2, pp. 311–314, 2003.

108. P. Marino, *The ICU Book*, Philadelphia, PA: Lippincott Williams and Wilkins, p. 365, 2013.

109. N. R. MacIntyre, "Respiratory Mechanics in the Patient Who Is Weaning from the Ventilator," *Respiratory Care*, vol. 50, no. 2, pp. 284–6, February 2005.

110. R. Chatburn, *Fundamentals of Mechanical Ventilation*, Mandu Press, 2003.

111. B. Cabello and J. Mancebo, "Work of Breathing," in *Applied Physiology in Intensive Care Medicine*, Berlin: Springer, 2006, p. 12.

112. P. N. Lanken, S. Manaker, B. A. Kohl, C. W. Hanson, III, *The Intensive Care Unit Manual*, Second ed. Saunders, an imprint of Elsevier, p. 254, 2015.

113. K. L. Yang and M. J. Tobin, "A Prospective Study of Indexes Predicting the Outcome of Trials of Weaning from Mechanical Ventilation," *The New England Journal of Medicine*, vol. 324, no. 21, pp. 1445–50, 1991.

114. K. Chomsky-Higgins and A. H. Harken, "Why Get Arterial Blood Gases?," in *Abernathy's Surgical Secrets (Seventh Edition)*, Elsevier, 2018.

115. T. Berger, J. Green, T. Horeczko, Y. Hagar, N. Garg, A. Suarez, E. Panacek, N. Shapiro, "Shock Index and Early Recognition of Sepsis in The Emergency Department: Pilot Study," *Western Journal of Emergency Medicine*, vol. 14, no. 2, pp. 168–74, 2013.

116. Deranged Physiology, "Static, Dynamic and Specific Compliance," [Online]. Available: https://derangedphysiology.com/main/cicm-primary-exam/required-reading/respiratory-system/Chapter%20031/static-dynamic-and-specific-compliance.

117. D. Limmer, M. F. O'Keefe and E. T. Dickenson, *Emergency Care*, 13th ed., Pearson, 2016.

118. A. S. Keller, L. L. Kirkland, S. Y. Rajasekaran, S. Cha, M. Y. Rady and J. M. Huddleston, "Unplanned Transfers to the Intensive Care Unit: The Role of the Shock Index," *Journal of Hospital Medicine*, vol. 5, no. 8, pp. 460–465, October 2010.

119. M. D. Buist, E. Jarmolowski, P. R. Burton, S. A. Bernard, B. P. Waxman and J. Anderson, "Recognising Clinical Instability in Hospital Patients Before Cardiac Arrest or Unplanned Admission to Intensive Care. A Pilot Study in a Tertiary-Care Hospital," *Medical Journal of Australia*, vol. 171, no. 1, pp. 22–25, 5 July 1999.

120. "Stroke - Medline Plus," US National Library of Medicine, [Online]. Available: https://medlineplus.gov/stroke.html.

121. W. Gobiet, W. Grote and W. J. Bock, "The Relation Between Intracranial Pressure, Mean Arterial Pressure and Cerebral Blood Flow in Patients with Severe Head Injury," *Acta Neurochirurgica*, vol. 32, no. 1–2, pp. 13–24, March 1975.

122. L. Hill and C. Gwinnutt, "Cerebral Blood Flow and Intracranial Pressure," [Online]. Available: http://www.frca.co.uk/Documents/170907%20Cerebral%20physiology%20I.pdf. [Accessed August 2019].

123. P. A. Blissitt, P. H. Mitchell, D. W. Newell, S. L. Woods and B. Belza, "Cerebrovascular Dynamics with Head-of-Bed Elevation in Patients with Mild or Moderate Vasospasm After Aneurysmal Subarachnoid Hemorrhage," *American Journal of Critical Care*, vol. 15, no. 2, pp. 206–216, March 2006.

124. Jamal Garah, Orly Eshach Adiv, Irit Rosen, Ron Shaoul. "The value of Integrated Pulmonary Index (IPI) monitoring during endoscopies in children." *J Clin Monit Comput* (2015) 29:773–7.

125. H. Mehta, R. Kashyap and S. Trivedi, "Correlation of End Tidal and Arterial Carbon Dioxide Levels in Critically Ill Neonates and Children," *Indian Journal of Critical Care Medicine*, vol. 18, no. 6, pp. 348–353, 2014.

Index

Note: Page numbers in *italics* denote tables and figures